PORSCHE

THE ROAD CARS

LAURENCE MEREDITH

SUTTON PUBLISHING

First published in the United Kingdom in 2000 by
Sutton Publishing Limited · Phoenix Mill · Thrupp · Stroud
Gloucestershire GL5 2BU

A catalogue record for this book is available from the British Library

ISBN 0 7509 2465 9

Typeset in 11/15 Baskerville.
Typesetting and origination by
Sutton Publishing Limited.
Printed and bound in England by
J.H. Haynes & Co. Ltd, Sparkford.

CONTENTS

INTRODUCTION

During the summer of 1999 I bumped into a friend, Linden Alcock; he told me that he was looking forward with great excitement to the Goodwood Festival of Speed, an annual event organised by Charles March. Linden felt sure that I would also be attending this huge motoring spectacle, because, as he pointed out, Goodwood had become the world's premier venue for seeing old cars 'in action', the famous people who drove them and for soaking up the motoring glories of days long since behind us.

I explained to my pal that I would not be going to Goodwood, because I had failed to understand what all the fuss was about. Despite having spent a lifetime at motor-racing circuits, I cannot identify with the Goodwood Festival, or the many similar events that now seem to capture the imagination of so many thousands of motoring enthusiasts.

I explained to Linden that, blessed, and burdened, with an accurate memory, I remember cars like the Lotus 25, Cooper T51, Porsche 906, Ferrari 512S and the rest when they were contemporary, state-of-the-art racing machines. Today, many of these cars have been 'over-restored' – to far 'better-than-new' condition – and are sometimes driven by amateurs who attempt to demonstrate their driving skill by stamping on the throttle pedal in a low gear and momentarily throwing the tail-end out of line.

Such 'spectacle' might provide thrills for some, but to me it is all rather sad, as this is not how it was. My chum Linden heavily criticised me for holding such a negative attitude. However, I maintain that while pretending to be Dan Gurney, Jacky Ickx, Juan Fangio, Jackie Stewart and Jim Clark is all very well, those who remember these true greats at work cannot really warm to the 'action' second time around. In writing this book, I have tried to convey a feeling for motoring as it actually was, particularly among the Porsche fraternity, and not in the manner of so many in today's old car movement who tend to view the past through thickly filtered rose-tinted spectacles.

After the Second World War the resumption of motor racing was a necessarily slow process. The first race was held in the Bois du Boulogne near Paris in September 1945. Low-key events followed in Britain and Italy, but Germans could not take part internationally until 1951. During the late 1940s motor racing was largely indulged by amateurs – 'clubbie' people with a thirst for speed and thrills. Many competed in pre-war cars, while others like Walter Glöckler of Germany built one-off specials based on VW Beetle components.

Many of the cars were crude, though effective, and no one cared about

Wheeling out old cars, like the fabulous Porsche-designed Auto-Union Grand-Prix machines of the 1930s, for modern events at Goodwood and elsewhere, is all well and good, but no motor racing spectacle of modern times can truly recapture the flavour and spirit of the original venues. Those who watched Rosemeyer, Müller, Stuck and Nuvolari conducting these massively powerful cars in action are understandably apt to describe modern racing cars as a trifle dull by comparison.

The Auto-Union Grand Prix cars of the 1930s were part of Adolf Hitler's scheme to demonstrate the supremacy of German engineering on the world's racing circuits. Porsche's future interests, however, lay in the production of sports cars, first with the 356 (left) and from 1964 with the 911. Both models were the products of innovation and engineering prowess, the classic rear-engined German machines standing the test of time like no other sports car – with the arguable exception of the British Morgan.

scratching the paintwork, if indeed there was paintwork to be scratched. Nobody polished alloy rocker covers to a mirror finish, nobody wasted champagne by spraying their fellow competitors. A racing car, whether a saloon, GT, sports or Grand Prix machine, was simply a car. It was not an automotive artefact to be polished and stored in a heated garage between auctions.

People went motor racing for serious fun, for there is not a known sport that is more exciting or exacting. By 1948, however, a number of manufacturers started to bring a degree of purpose into competition. They included Porsche, Ferrari, Jaguar and Aston Martin, who 'conspired' to build sports cars that for many future years would compete in races that have become the backbone of motorsport, and to be responsible for the development of road cars. Daimler-Benz would join this fray in 1951 – the first year in which Porsche entered cars for the Le Mans 24 Hours – and win Le Mans comprehensively in 1952.

During the 1950s Grand Prix racing became the specialist preserve of Alfa-Romeo, Ferrari, Maserati, Daimler-Benz, Lancia, Vanwall and Cooper, who took part in races supported by also-rans like Lago-Talbot, Gordini, HWM, OSCA and the ill-fated BRM. Sports cars, sports racers and Grand Touring machines, with which the car-buying public could more closely and readily identify, were much more diversified and varied.

To many these cars were also infinitely more interesting because of their versatility. A Porsche 356, for example, could be used for shopping, touring, rallying and circuit racing. A Vanwall, by contrast, could only be driven in a Grand Prix, which sadly meant that it would spend long periods of time between races merely sitting – doing nothing – on the concrete floor of a workshop. A car such as the Vanwall also demanded to be driven by a skilled professional like

(Sir) Stirling Moss, for example, whereas almost anyone could jump behind the wheel of a Porsche 356 and have fun.

From its inception, or more accurately its rejuvenation, in 1948, Porsche of Zuffenhausen has concentrated its efforts predominantly on the production of sports cars for road use. This book is about Porsche's road cars, but the term 'road cars' requires qualifying, because throughout Porsche's history there has always been an overlap between machines constructed for driving on the road and those intended as pukka racing cars. The distinction between the two types is very blurred, even in recent times.

A simple example will suffice. In 1996 Porsche built the GT1, a high-tech machine developing 600bhp intended as a track challenger to the Gordon Murray designed McLaren F1. Astonishingly fast and breathtakingly beautiful, the GT1's principal role was as a competitor in international sports-car racing. Distinguished externally with a 'dorsal' engine air scoop and massive rear wing, it was not originally envisaged as a car for everyday driving on public roads. However, true to the company's roots, a slightly detuned street version is available to the lucky few with sufficiently healthy bank accounts.

What constitutes a Porsche road car is also difficult to determine because of the many circuits on which sports-car races are held. The Le Mans 24 Hours is the greatest and most important race on the annual calendar, yet much of the Sarthe circuit is made up of public roads. During the 1950s and 1960s legendary competitions like the Targa Florio and Mille Miglia were held exclusively on public roads, and manufacturers such as Porsche built cars to withstand the many obstacles – cobbled streets for instance – that were not features of smooth tarmac, venues like the old airfield at Silverstone.

In 1953 Porsche built its first pukka sports racing car, the 550. Powered at first by the 1.5-litre pushrod engine, and later the Furhmann-designed four-cam unit, these cars developed a reputation as 'giant-killers', particularly in events like the Targa Florio in Sicily. In the tradition of all great sports racing cars of this era, though, the 550 was capable of being driven quite easily on public roads – and many were. Unhappily, it was in one of these cars that the Hollywood film actor James Dean lost his life in September 1955.

Until 1965 the staple model of the Porsche line-up was the 356; built alongside this production car were the racing machines, many of which were also made available to selected private customers. The latter were perfectly at home on public roads, as indeed they had to be, for they not only competed in events like the Targa, but were driven to and from such venues as well.

Great events like the Panamericana Mexico, Tour of Sicily, Tour de France, Mille Miglia and Targa Florio have long since passed into history, thanks to those people who consider them to be too dangerous, and as a result there is no need for competition cars to be usable under road conditions. These vehicles have become more specialised, as they are largely confined to closed circuits, but this has not prevented Porsche (and others) from producing cars that can be driven on both road and track.

It is clear, however, that the carefree, simple days of motor racing have gone for ever, which is most regrettable. If forty people lose their lives during an avalanche while skiing in the alps, the world's media speaks and writes, quite rightly, of a tragedy. If one person dies in a motor-racing accident, though, there are calls for this 'dangerous' sport to be banned, which is not correct. On this basis it is not difficult to understand the reasons for the motorsport fraternity protecting itself from fools by taking to clinically safe circuits where risks are minimised.

Things were not always so dull, as the late Denis Jenkinson pointed out in his book, *Porsche Past and Present* (Gentry Books). 'Jenks' commented:

> One nice thing about the Targa Florio races in Sicily during the 1950s and 1960s was that the competing cars were proper two-seater sports/racing cars, and were driven from the garages and workshops to

the circuit for both practice and the race. This meant that you could always get a ride in one of the cars if you talked nicely to the team manager or the head mechanic. For a number of years I used to stay at the Hotel San Lucia in Cefalu, a few miles to the east of the circuit, and the Porsche works team also stayed there, using the large underground garage as a workshop in which to prepare the cars. Providing you were up bright and early, and were ready to go, it was possible to ride to the circuit in the passenger's seat. In 1960, when Porsche were running the Spyder RS60 cars, I got a lift with Hubert Mimmler, the head mechanic, in the car Joakim Bonnier was to race.

'Cadging a lift' in, or driving, a car like the Spyder RS60 was a possibility for almost normal mortals in those days, and such fun continued at Porsche until the mid-1960s, by which time the motoring world was beginning to change out of all traditional recognition. Conventional wisdom argues forcefully that the last Porsche sports racing car that could be driven on public roads was the 904 of 1965. There is a point to this, of course, but many of the racing cars built after this date are included in this book because they were also driven on public roads, and sported registration plates to prove it!

After series production of the evergreen 911 got underway in 1964, this model formed the basis of Porsche's road cars. With development the 911, in its many varied guises, became a more powerful proposition than the pukka prototype racing cars of the late 1960s and beyond.

The 904 of 1964/65 was the last Porsche sports racing car that could be used in competition and as a road car. It was also the first Porsche with bodywork made of fibreglass. Designed by Ferry Porsche's eldest son Butzi it was hailed as a styling masterpiece. Fitted with the 2-litre, four-cam engine, the 904 was perfectly tractable in the rough and tumble of everyday road driving, but high noise levels in the cabin made for wearying long-distance journeys.

The GT2 911, for example, produced from 1995, is a perfectly usable road car, yet it has a higher top speed, and is appreciably quicker around a racing circuit, than a good many of Porsche's sports racing cars from the late 1960s. I reiterate, therefore, that the distinction between Porsche's road and racing machines has always been blurred.

There was a time not long ago that Grand Prix machines were frequently driven on public roads. Such activity was as illegal then as it is now, but things were different in the 1950s and 1960s. Grand Prix races were great sporting occasions – today they are not – and duty policeman did everything they could to ensure that the racing cars got to the circuit on time. If a Ferrari needed a high-speed blast down the motorway prior to a race, the authorities quietly closed the road for a short time; Ferrari is after all part of Italy's heritage. Today, this would result in endless police investigations, the imposition of heavy fines on the offending parties, grossly misleading headlines in the international press and approving smirks on the faces of the *tifosi*.

As Grand Prix and American CART racing have become more rarified and specialised, sports-car manufacturers have largely kept faith with the true spirit of motor racing. Jaguar, Sauber, Mercedes-Benz, Peugeot, Rondeau, Spice, Lancia, Porsche, of course, Ecosse, Aston Martin, Ferrari, McLaren and many others have all in recent times flown the sports-car flag – many with componentry derived and developed in road cars.

In 1982 Porsche debuted the glorious 956, a special sports prototype for the inaugural Group C Championship. Developing well in excess of 600bhp, the 956, and 962 derivative, was an out-and-out track racer – the most successful sports racing car ever – but this did not prevent Vern Schuppan and Jochen Dauer building road-legal versions.

During the course of writing this book the world entered a new millennium, and a new age in which technological progress will result in truly astonishing discoveries. The fields of information technology, genetics, space travel, medicine, farming and automotive engineering will dramatically change the lives of everyone on the planet during the twenty-first century. Looking at the many hundreds of pictures I rifled from Porsche's archive for the purpose of illustrating this book was just one personal way in which I was able to take stock of the twentieth century during the millennium celebrations.

For old 'codgers' of my aged generation it is almost unthinkable that the first car to bear the Porsche family name was produced more than half a century ago. Almost the same period of time has elapsed since Butzi Porsche laid down the initial designs for the 911, and more than thirty years have passed since Porsche scored its first outright victory at Le Mans. It all seems like yesterday, but it wasn't!

Much has been learnt in the automotive world during the last twenty-five years of the twentieth century. Today's racing cars are no faster in a straight line, but they are a good deal safer, go round corners much more quickly and stop more efficiently. Travelling on public roads in a fast sports car is no longer the pleasure it once was, due to increasing traffic density and stifling road regulations. Looking back to Porsche's formative years, and the days in which it became the world's most successful and dominant sports-car manufacturer, therefore, is not only interesting but serves as a timely reminder that progress does not always result in improvement – as everyone interested in old cars is only too well aware.

Laurence Meredith
January 2000

The author's favourite Porsche, the gaspingly beautiful 906, or Carrera 6, superseded the 904 in 1966, and was largely the work of Dr Piëch. By the mid-1960s sports-car racing had become so specialised that the 906 could not be driven to and from a sporting event. With its 911-derived, six-cylinder engine developing 210bhp, the 906 was a fast, purpose-built racer that put the Stuttgart concern on the road to its ultimate goal – overall victory at Le Mans.

Photographed here in short-tail form, the 917, first launched in 1969, gave Porsche its first Le Mans victory in 1970. Once described by Derek Bell as the world's 'most outrageous motor car', the 917 was capable of well in excess of 240mph, its 4.5- and 5-litre engines developing in the region of 600bhp. In no way could the 917 ever be described as a suitable sports car for road use, but this did not prevent Count Rossi of the Martini drinks empire from registering his example for the road.

Chapter 1

356 – FROM SAWMILL TO STUTTGART

The foundations for Porsche's first sports car, built in 1948, can be traced directly to the Porsche Type 64 Berlin racer. One of three similar cars built in 1939 for the stillborn Berlin–Rome road race, it was based on Volkswagen components and fitted with a low-drag aluminium bodyshell. It was in this car that Professor Porsche and his chauffeur Goldinger once averaged 81mph between Fallersleben, near Wolfsburg, and Berlin. In 1998, this author, driving a modern turbocharged Volkswagen, could manage an average speed of no more than 51mph over the same stretch of autobahn. Such is the price and pace of 'progress'.

Introduction

In 1999 Porsche quietly celebrated its best-ever financial year, had roughly 8,000 people on the company's payroll and stepped into the third millennium with a strong degree of optimisim. Until Adolf Hitler's troops started decisively attacking the Poles in the late summer of 1939, Ferdinand Porsche also had reason to be optimistic, for the venerable professor and his small team of designers and engineers had successfully completed the construction of three important cars.

Based on VW Beetle components and clothed in a streamlined alloy body, these handsome machines – codenamed the Porsche Type 60K10 – were intended to compete in the stillborn Berlin–Rome road race. Fitted with a 1.5-litre version of the Volkswagen air-cooled flat-four, the car was good for a top speed of 90mph and, with its four wheels independently sprung by torsion bars, had the cornering agility of the most corrupt of politicians.

The Berlin–Rome race was intended as an event that would, in some way or other, galvanise the dubious political relationship between Hitler and the Italian dictator Benito Mussolini. Predictably, there were squabbles between the two nations as to where the race should start and end, but the arguing was all rather academic. Britain's prime minister, Neville Chamberlain, was not interested in motor racing and, having been accurately warned by Winston Churchill for the previous two years of Hitler's plans for global domination, promptly declared war on Germany.

The advent of the Second World War scuppered plans for the great road race, and Porsche's three cars immediately became obsolete. Regrettably, only one of the 'Berlin' cars survives, and has been campaigned in historic events in recent years by Otto Mathé. It is this car, and its two similar sisters, to which the company largely owes its current success. Its low-drag body, rear-mounted, horizontally opposed engine and unique chassis were established as Porsche hallmarks that remain intact today.

As Germany's foremost engineering designer, Porsche spent the dark years between 1939 and 1945 draughting and building machines for military purposes, with almost inevitable consequences. Incorrectly branded as a war 'criminal', the old man and his son Ferry were unjustly incarcerated in a French prison, and it fell to the professor's daughter Louise Piëch to steer the remains of the Porsche company through the 'rubble' in the aftermath of the Second World War.

Ferry gained his freedom ahead of his father and by 1947 had once again found his feet. He was every bit as talented as his father and, like the majority of Germanic people to this day, recognised the virtues of hard work. In June 1947 Ferry and his small team began initial work on Porsche's 349th design – which became known as the 356 – as the company's first design for Wanderer in 1931 was officially numbered the seventh.

This first prototype (chassis number 356-001) debuted as a rolling chassis in March 1948. Designed by Erwin Komenda, also the architect of the Beetle's definitive shape, the Porsche's bodywork would take a little longer to create. Porsche's faithful bodymaker Friedrich Weber was a highly skilled craftsman, but was apt to be under the influence of alcohol for long periods, and could not return to work until he was good, ready and sober. Interestingly, the legendary Merdardo Fantuzzi, who built bodies for Ferrari and Maserati racing cars during the 1950s and 1960s, had a similar addiction to food, and a most impressive waistline to prove it.

Porsche's first sports car was a strict two-seater, with a shapely alloy open body sitting atop a Volkswagen chassis and running gear. The 1131cc Beetle engine was mounted amidships with the gearbox behind the rear axle line – the opposite of the Beetle's arrangement. With twin Solex carburettors and the compression ratio raised from 5.8:1 to 7:1, power output was a feeble 40bhp, but an increase of 15bhp over the standard Beetle's unit.

With little money for developing special components, the car's entire mechanical package was sourced from Volkswagen's factory at Wolfsburg. For comparatively little financial outlay Porsche had a lightweight sports car capable of 80mph with great potential. The car made its press debut at the Swiss Grand Prix on 8 June 1948, and just over a month later Ferry Porsche's cousin, Herbert Kaes (also Ferdinand Porsche's secretary), took the car to its first victory in a road race at Innsbruck.

At this stage the company was based in Gmünd, Austria, which was far from ideal. The premises, an old sawmill, were cramped, the supply of raw materials was difficult and rail communications were almost non-existent. However, throughout 1949 Porsche and his people beavered away with their cache of hand tools and built the first examples of the 356. Because of the lack of luggage space and seating capacity in the mid-engined prototype, all subsequent 356s were rear-engined in Beetle fashion, which allowed for the inclusion of a small seat in the rear.

The coupe and cabriolet continued to be made of alloy, and were handmade, of course, but the build process was slow and uneconomical. Ferry Porsche solved this by establishing new premises at Zuffenhausen, a small suburb of Stuttgart, where series production began in 1950. Production of the Gmünd cars continued until 1951, but was halted after the forty-ninth example had been completed. Cars built at Stuttgart differed most significantly in having bodies constructed of steel by the Reutter coachworks, which was situated next door to the Porsche factory.

It was originally envisaged that demand for the new car would not exceed 500 examples in total. What Ferry Porsche's plans were for the future after this arbitrary figure had been completed is anyone's guess, but this serves to illustrate that even people of Porsche's great stature occasionally make mistakes.

When the Porsche 356 made its public debut at the Geneva Motor Show in 1949 sales were already well under way, and press reaction had been most favourable. The car was far from conventional, extremely well made, had good traction and roadholding properties and, considering the diminutive engine capacity, had reasonably good performance.

An agreement between Ferry Porsche and Volkswagen's chief executive Heinz Nordhoff had secured a regular supply of parts for the fledgling sports-car concern, but performance development was well under way in 1951 and so was the company's long-held ambition to participate in international motorsport. As the years wore on fewer and fewer VW components would feature in Porsche's sports cars!

Porsche's international competition debut, the 1951 Le Mans 24 Hours, started with good intentions, with four cars being prepared for the event. However, three of them were demolished prior to the start in silly accidents. This left a lone entry of an 1100cc, alloy bodied, Gmünd-built car for the French pairing of Veuillet/Mouche. To reduce aerodynamic drag the car's wheel arches were enclosed, and the diminutive Porsche circulated for the 24 hours at an average speed of 74mph, completing several laps at an average of 87mph, which was sufficient to attain a class win and twentieth place overall. Equally important, this success assured Porsche of an entry in the following year's French endurance race.

There was a great deal of publicity about Porsche following the 1951 outing, and sales of road cars escalated. By the end of 1951 the production cars were available in several different states of tune, with a choice of 1.1-, 1.3- (44bhp) and 1.5-litre (55bhp and 72bhp) engines. The 1.3- and 1.5-litre units were also made available with either plain crankshaft bearings or Hirth-supplied crankshafts with roller bearings, the latter being intended mainly for use in competition.

In August 1951 Paul von Guilleaume and Count von der Muhler in a 1500 356 achieved a class win and third overall in the Liège–Rome–Liège Rally. A little later in the same year Porsche took a 72bhp 1500, with larger carburettors and a reprofiled camshaft, to Montlhéry, set eleven new international speed records (for 1500cc cars) and a world record for 72 hours with an average speed of 95.2mph.

In 1952 Veuillet and Mouche again won their class at Le Mans, and Prince Metternich took his cabriolet 356 to eighth overall in the Carrera Panamericana road race in Mexico, which was most impressive considering that the Ferraris, Maseratis and Mercedes in front of him had double the engine capacity. By this time Porsche was enjoying considerable success; after the 356's 'crash' gearbox was replaced with a synchromesh unit in October 1952 it became a sports car of real desire, especially for those who had never mastered the art of silent gear changing and double-declutching.

By March 1951 Porsche had produced its 500th 356. Almost exactly five years later, in March 1956, the 10,000th production car had been completed, which finally awakened Ferry Porsche to the indisputable fact that his car was considerably better than even he had suspected. However, the Porsche was not without its critics, who argued that a 'proper' sports car had its engine in the 'correct' place – up front – was fitted with sparkling wire wheels and had bodywork painted in British Racing Green. Many were sneering about the funny rear-engined car from Stuttgart.

During the 1950s construction of traditional sports cars was almost the sole preserve of the British and Italians. There were cheap and cheerless cars like those from MG, Morgan, Triumph and Alfa-Romeo on the one hand, and more powerful offerings from Jaguar, Austin-Healey, Ferrari and Maserati on the other. In terms of engineering integrity, sophistication and road ability not one of these even came close to BMW's pre-war 328, and British manufacturers in particular continued for years with their outdated wares in the complacent belief that Coventry was the car capital of the world.

By the mid-1950s both Porsche and Daimler-Benz had risen to the forefront of innovative, modern design, while British manufacturers stood still with their eyes firmly shut. The Porsche 356 had built up an international following of discerning car enthusiasts, who appreciated the car's performance, handling and almost unrivalled build quality. It also came as a shock to many that, in contrast to the majority of

British cars of the 1950s, the Porsche's engine would run for years without requiring major mechanical surgery.

From a comparatively early stage in the development of the 356, Porsche had the wit to recognise the importance of the American market. Young people in particular in this great country had money to spend, and were hungry for exciting sports cars. Porsche would pull out the stops to oblige them, and throughout 1952 produced the Type 540, or America Roadster. These were open-top two-seaters with aluminium bodies built by Heuer. Intended for club competition use, the Roadster had a rudimentary soft-top, detachable windscreen, lightweight aluminium-framed seats and leather bonnet straps. By stripping the car of unnecessary equipment the Roadster could quickly shed 115lb of superfluous weight. Fitted with the 75bhp 1500cc engine, it was appreciably quicker than the regular steel-bodied 356 and, like so many subsequent Porsches, was capable of showing a clean pair of heels to rivals with much larger capacity engines. Unfortunately, only sixteen examples of the America Roadster were completed before the Heuer concern went bust.

However, the company would take the concept a step further in 1954. At the suggestion of Max Hoffmann, the Austrian-born, America-based car dealer, the company built the Speedster, a 'no-frills', lightweight version of the 356 Cabriolet. With revised styling the bodies were built by Beutler, and the concept was based on the America Roadster's; this was intended as a sports car that could be driven to a race meeting, stripped of unnecessary equipment, thrashed for several laps and driven home again. In standard form it had a much shorter windscreen than the regular 356, detachable sidescreens instead of 'wind-up' windows and hip-hugging bucket seats. The dashboard also sported a 'humped' binnacle with three circular instruments, and there was the usual, bewildering choice of power units. These included 1300 Normal and Supers, plain-bearing 1500 and, after the debut of the 356A in 1955, a choice of 60bhp Normal or 75bhp Super engines.

The 356A was introduced at the 1955 Frankfurt Auto Show, and although to the same basic design, was a far more civilised car than the original concept. The road wheels were reduced from 16 in to 15 in, the wheel arches became more rounded, the 'V'-shaped windscreen was changed for a more modern panoramic piece and the headlining was changed from cloth to vinyl to give a contemporary and bright ambience to the interior.

Although the 44bhp and 60bhp 1300 engines continued in production, the new 1600 unit provided a welcome increase in power over the outgoing 1500cc engine. In Normal plain-bearing guise there was 60bhp available from the 1600, whereas the same engine with a roller-bearing crankshaft in the Super version pushed out 75bhp.

The model range comprised the coupe, cabriolet and Speedster, and also from 1955 there were Carrera versions of the Speedster and coupe. Carrera – Spanish for 'race' – was adopted after the company's success in the Carrera Panamericana road races in Mexico, and defined the company's range-topping model. This car was distinguished externally by Carrera badging on the tail, but it was the power unit located there that really gave the game away.

Work started on this new engine in 1950, and was distinguished from the regular production power units by its four overhead camshafts in place of pushrods actuated by a single camshaft. The work of Dr Ernst Fuhrmann – his *magnum opus* – the engine was first used in a 550 sports racing car (of which more later) at the Nürburgring in 1953. Porsche tried to keep this engine a secret, but those present at the Nürburgring on that occasion were not fooled, for the exhaust note was markedly different from the regular unit's.

In its original 1500cc form the 'four-cammer', as it became popularly known, developed 100bhp at 6,200rpm and was officially launched at the Paris Motor Show in autumn 1953. In 1954 a Porsche 550 fitted with the four-cam engine scored sixth place and a class win in the Mille Miglia, and later in the same year a similar car finished third overall and scored a class victory in the Panamericana road race.

Naturally, the 356 Carreras made for formidable road cars. Their roller-bearing crankshafts endowed the engines with a free-revving smoothness that simply did not exist in other contemporary sports cars. Power delivery was smooth, the engine safe to 7,000rpm and a top speed of 125mph was easily on the cards. Denis Jenkinson once took a works Carrera in racing trim for a run around Stuttgart and, apart from enjoying a 'terrific surge' of power up to 100mph, considered it to be among the most user-friendly sports machines of its day. 'Jenks' commented:

The [tachometer] needle whizzed round to 7,500rpm phenomenally quickly, with that lovely hard noise from the engine, the firm push on the back of the seat and a gear change that was as quick as you could move the lever. After many laps of the Solitude, which is one of my favourite circuits, I then went off into the lovely countryside south of Stuttgart for some 'fast touring', before returning by way of the autobahn for a last glorious blast as far as the Zuffenhausen turn-off. In spite of being to racing specification, the car was entirely flexible and docile and poodled back into Zuffenhausen and round to the back of the racing department like a Volkswagen. That was fun.

Like the regular 356, Carreras were developed all the way to their demise in 1965. A lightweight GT version became available in 1957 with Perspex windows, aluminium doors and a host of other features compatible with motor-racing requirements. The four-cam 1500 engine was enlarged to 1600 (from 1958) and to 2 litres (from 1962), the final incarnation marking the ultimate development of the four-cylinder power unit within the parameters of 1960s engineering know-how.

Carreras, however, were extremely expensive to buy, particularly in Britain, where goverment-imposed taxes bumped up the price artificially. They were, therefore, comparatively rare. The regular range was also far from cheap, but this did not prevent a year-on-year rise in sales figures. Porsche's increasingly loyal customers recognised the superior quality of the Zuffenhausen car and were clearly prepared to fork out for quality. In Britain dozens of 'converts' to the Porsche fold were simply fed up with being let down, time and again, by products of the indigenous motor industry.

In 1957 Porsche announced the T2 version of the 356A, which had a number of detail changes. These included teardrop-shaped rear lights (actually introduced in March 1957), modified door handles, tail-pipes that passed through the bumper, revised interior courtesy lamps, 'tunnel-type' gearbox casing and a ZF worm-and-peg steering gearbox. At this stage the car had been in series production for seven years, equal to the length of time that one model remains in production today. However, Porsche were never in the habit of making modifications for the sake of it, and the 356A continued until 1959 when it was superseded by the 'facelifted' 356B, or T5. The new model was outwardly similar, the majority of alterations being 'sub-cutaneous' in traditional German fashion. External changes included larger bumpers, which resulted in the headlamps and taillights being mounted higher on the wings, a bonnet with a wider leading edge and a broader, longer handle. The T6 launched two years later was revised again; this also had a wider front lid and larger window glass, and there were twin air-intakes on the expanded rear lid.

In addition to the two regular 60bhp and 75bhp 1600 engines, the 356B saw the introduction of the 1600 Super 90 (90bhp) unit. The additional power was achieved with larger, twin-choke Solex P11-4 twin carburettors, increased diameter inlet valves and revised cylinder heads that improved the flow of the fuel/air mixture. Naturally, valve actuation was by pushrods, rather than overhead camshafts, which kept everything nice and simple when it came to servicing and maintenance. In this modified form the 1600cc Super 90 was good for a top speed of about 110mph, or roughly equal to the fuel-injected, 1.6-litre Volkswagen Golf GTi of the mid-1970s and beyond.

By the beginning of the 1960s, Porsche's little cars had begun to enjoy huge success in GT and sports-car racing. Owners of the pure road cars identified closely with this success, as their vehicles were little different from racing versions. Although the company was banking healthy profits at this time, it, like all successful German companies, invested heavily in future projects. In keeping with his customers, Ferry Porsche drove himself in a 356; he was not chauffeured in a Mercedes-Benz limousine, and many contemporary captains of British industry would have done well to have copied his example.

During the latter half of the 1950s the top prizes in international sports-car racing were earned by Jaguar, Maserati and Ferrari. Porsche were particularly successful in events like the Targa Florio, where chassis agility paid dividends over 'brute force and bloody ignorance', but success in the big events, such as Daytona and Le Mans, was never on the cards. With their diminutive 1.5- and 1.6-litre engines, the 356s and sports racers were never far behind, but simply lacked top-end 'grunt' to stay with the big players like Enzo Ferrari. Numerous class wins brought healthy publicity, but victory at the most significant event – Le Mans – would remain elusive for some time.

On both sides of the Atlantic the 356's following gathered at an astonishing pace; drivers would greet each other on the roads with a friendly wave and flash of headlamps. Porsche ownership was a strong conversation opener, and enthusiastic clubs were formed to ensure that the dialogue continued. In the USA, particularly California, the austere Speedster had reigned supreme as the 'smart' car of the mid-1950s.

This highly sought-after machine was replaced by the slightly more luxurious Convertible D in late 1957 (twenty-five Carrera Speedsters with 1600cc, four-cam engines were built in 1959), and there was a new Roadster version from 1958. The latter was in the same spirit as the Speedster, but came with the convenience of a 'full-size' windscreen, improved headroom, wind-up windows and even a cigar lighter. For owners of the Speedster, Convertible D and Roadster, the factory also supplied fibreglass hard-tops at extra cost. These were eminently practical and easy to fit, but are of such doubtful aesthetic appeal that they are especially rare today.

At the beginning of the 1960s large sections of the automotive industry were booming, and looking forward to capitalising on the new-found wealth of an emergent middle class. In 1961 Jaguar launched the glamorous 149mph, 4.2-litre E-Type, Ferrari were on a winning streak in top-level sports-car racing, and would continue to be victorious until 1965 when Ford finally decided that Enzo had had his own way for far too long, and Porsche entered the dizzy world of Formula 1.

Apart from victories by American ace Dan Gurney at the French Grand Prix and a non-championship round at Solitude a fortnight later, Porsche's Grand Prix foray was a disaster. The eight-cylinder car was flattered by Gurney's driving ability, and the project was closed down for good at the end of the 1962 season. Porsche were established as manufacturers of sports cars – it is what they did best – and the company's efforts would remain largely in this field for many, many years.

Luckily, the 356 continued to sell well, despite the failure of the F1 project. Porsche's sports racing cars continued to be successful, and this mattered above all else. However, as this new decade wore on, Porsche, like so many other manufacturers, had to contend with a new breed of journalists, who were not of the same sycophantic persuasion as their predecessors. Fine points of criticism began to increase as the motoring world became ever more discerning, and journalists took the view that if manufacturers expected to make big profits, the car-buying public had a right to expect better and better machines.

Criticism of Porsche's products was aimed principally at the relatively high purchase price, the clatter of the air-cooled, flat-four power unit and the car's handling characteristics. A 1600cc 356 cost as much as a 4.2-litre E-Type Jaguar; Porsche owners knew the difference in quality between the two cars and remained happy to pay for the Zuffenhausen machine. The majority also loved the unique sound of the engine, but the vitriol aimed at the handling characteristics would not go away.

As all dyed-in-the-wool Porsche people know, there is nothing wrong with the Porsche's handling, once the unique driving technique has been mastered. So many journalists failed to appreciate that the car's inherent tendency to oversteer, at and beyond the limit of tyre adhesion, was a facet to be exploited and enjoyed. One great characteristic of the swing-axle rear suspension was its predictability. It gave advanced warning of the tail stepping out of line long before this actually happened, which is why skilled drivers prepared themselves for, and revelled in, the delights of opposite-lock motoring. Those who failed to master the technique, in complete ignorance, branded the Porsche's handling as 'unsatisfactory', or even 'dangerous'.

Of the car's roadholding Denis Jenkinson commented: 'With the pushrod-engined Porsches, you could flatten the throttle pedal round most bends with no qualms at all, but in the Carrera we had to drive more circumspectly and with better precision, for it had nearly twice the horsepower with not much more weight. You could easily get throttle happy and spin, but although we had some hectic moments, we always managed to get back under control.'

Really skilled drivers took to Porsches in droves, for it was a car that brought out the best in driving skill. The difference between a skilled person and one of average ability was so transparently demonstrated at the 1958 Six Hour Relay Race at Silverstone, when the late Jimmy Clark, driving a 1600S 356, regularly lapped the old club circuit in 2 minutes 4 seconds. By contrast, the well-known amateur driver and Porsche enthusiast Jack Burke could manage no better than 2 minutes 12 seconds in his much more powerful Carrera. Jim Clark's performance on this occasion did nothing to harm sales of the 356 in Britain but, by the beginning of the 1960s, Porsche had become fitful that the car had been in production for a long time, and work therefore began on a successor.

In 1963, the much-loved 356 received its final 'facelift', and was relaunched as the 356C. Styling kept faith with the T6 bodyshell of 1961, as it was aerodynamically proven and there was no need to change it. There were small alterations to the internal switchgear, the seats were reshaped for improved lateral support and engine choice was limited to two reworked 1600cc pushrod units – 75bhp and 95bhp in the 'C' and 'SC' models respectively – and the 2-litre four-cam Carrera.

The most significant modification to the new model, however, was the adoption of all-round disc brakes. Braking was the only area of automotive engineering in which German manufacturers lagged well behind their British counterparts. While Porsche and Daimler-Benz had used alloy cased and ribbed brake drums on their road and racing cars throughout the 1950s, Jaguar had the huge advantage of discs, which the Coventry firm had developed in conjunction with Dunlop. With the ability to dissipate heat much faster than drums, their efficiency was beyond question, and although the first 200 or so 356Cs continued to be fitted with drums, subsequent Porsches had all-round discs. Largely thanks to Daimler-Benz's chief development engineer, Rudi Uhlenhaut, radial tyres had also been perfected by this time, and these were fitted to the Porsche as standard wear. Naturally, they transformed both the roadholding and handling qualities of the 356, as anyone who has reverted to crossplies will be aware.

By 1963, though, the writing was on the wall for the 356. In this same year Porsche had debuted the six-cylinder 901, or 911 as it would become known, and Daimler-Benz started production of another fine six-cylinder car, the 230SL 'Pagoda'. Towards the end of its days the 356 no longer shared any components with the Volkswagen Beetle, and had a reputation as one of the world's finest all-round sports-cum-GT machines. Its build quality was only rivalled by Daimler-Benz's fine products, and the Porsche undoubtedly had the world's second-best synchromesh gearbox. The very finest was fitted to the VW Beetle . . . and still is! Neither the Porsche nor Mercedes-Benz 230SL had the glamour of a Ferrari, Maserati or Lamborghini, but on the side of the German cars were proven reliability, advanced chassis engineering, excellent fuel consumption and longevity.

It appeared that Porsche just could not put a foot wrong. By the early 1960s the company had established itself as a manufacturer of excellent sports and sports racing cars (and high-quality tractors!) and as a consultant to the motor industry in general. After its test facility at Weissach was completed, Porsche's services were much in demand from other manufacturers. Porsche's engineers and designers were enlisted by several companies to assist on a huge variety of projects. There were new designs for Volkswagen, aimed at replacing the Beetle, for Studebaker in the USA, and prototype work for many others. In 1964, the company acquired the Reutter coachbuilders (now seatmakers, Recaro) and put the 901 into series production.

Many of the people who had become part of the world's 356 fraternity loathed the 901/911 replacement model at first, but their views had been both calculated and expected by the canny Ferry Porsche. He was of the opinion that instant positive reaction was never likely to last; the 911, he thought, would 'grow' on the Porsche-buying public, and he was absolutely right. To appease enthusiasts of the 356, though, production continued alongside the 911 until 1965, and a small number were also built in 1966.

By the mid-1960s there was no shortage of choice in the sports-car market. At the relatively inexpensive end there were crude machines like the Triumph TR, MGB and 'Spridget' and Morgan. One or two rungs up were Alfa-Romeo, Jaguar and Jensen, and at the top of the tree were the Astons, Ferraris, Maseratis and Lamborghinis. All of these cars were powered by water-cooled, multi-cylinder engines, positioned up front, driving the rear wheels. Porsche, by contrast, forged a lonely path with air-cooled engines positioned in the tail. Of all these manufacturers, only Morgan and Porsche survive as independents. Without exception the others have been taken over by larger concerns, or gone out of business altogether, which surely serves as a lesson in the virtues of long-term planning.

From roughly 1965 the world in general began, for good and ill, to change. Those who could not keep up with, or stay ahead of, this movement would fall by the wayside. Many did. By 1967 that great British sports car, the Healey 3000, became extinct. With little will to adapt the car to the demands of American legislation it was sadly allowed to die. Porsche, however, dealt with new situations in a more intelligent manner.

The 356 was a great car of the 1950s, and is perceived as such today, but Porsche could not rely on nostalgia and human affection for useful inanimate objects if it was also to face up to the responsibility it owed to its many employees. First and foremost the people working in Zuffenhausen were engineers and, as Ferry Porsche was often at pains to point out, engineers should always try to solve problems in the simplest possible way. In 1964 this meant waving goodbye to the old car, and making way for a new and much more sophisticated machine, which was aimed at a clientele that had also become considerably more suave.

From the original 1.1-litre cars of the early days to the 2-litre four-cam Carreras of the 1960s, the Porsche 356 had enjoyed seventeen years of considerable development. It had become a classic, in the true sense, but the best days lay ahead with a car that all but the foolish and ignorant would recognise as the world's best all-round sports car.

A unique Porsche, this diesel-engined Type 60 was built in 1950 as a 'one-off'. Although economical, the diesel power unit proved to be under-powered and the project was shelved. The Volkswagen Beetle was, of course, THE motoring icon of the twentieth century, and arguably represented Professor Porsche's greatest of many masterpieces. This is the car that the Rootes Group once described in an official report as 'some kind of joke'.

The first sports car to bear the famous Porsche name was completed by 1948, and differed from the production 356s in that it was mid-engined. An open two-seater, this prototype, seen here in Gmünd, Austria, had a tuned, twin-carburettor Beetle engine, and a lightweight, aluminium-alloy body built by Friedrich Weber.

To achieve the mid-engined layout, the prototype's Beetle power unit and gearbox were simply turned through 180 degrees, which inevitably led to the gearbox being slung out in the tail. In this shot the small, 6-volt starter motor, bolted to the left-hand side of the gearbox, and shock absorber mounting are clearly visible – and most accessible for servicing and maintenance. Mounted at the rear of the engine compartment, the spare wheel is fitted with an absurdly narrow crossply tyre, but was entirely in keeping with contemporary thinking.

Finished in the classic German colour combination of silver with red leather seats, the prototype's cabin is a model of post-war simplicity and austerity. Dashboard instrumentation is minimal, the spoked steering wheel a hangover from the 1930s, and the two-piece wind deflector is the functional result of corporate impecuniosity, but there is no denying the car's primary purpose as a pure sports car.

By 1952 the Porsche prototype had passed into the hands of Hermann Schulthess (the car's third owner), seen here with members of his family. By this stage the car had been slightly modified; in this shot the shape of the rear wings has clearly been altered, and there are vented 356 wheels at the front. If nothing else, this archive picture illustrates that it is possible to squash seven people into a two-seater sports car.

By 1953, when this shot was taken at Gedachtnisfahrt, Salzburg, the prototype's bodywork had been further modified, with upswept wings front and rear and all four wheels being of the vented type. Owner Hermann Schultess is in the driving seat, with a happy, smiling Louise Piëch – Ferry Porsche's sister – perched on the rear bulkhead. Note the brace of 356 coupes, Beetle cabriolet and Volkswagen Transporter in the background.

A sports car for fast continental motoring, or club-style competition, in full flight. By today's standards the prototype's top speed of a shade under 90mph is little to get excited about, but considering the few resources available to the Porsche team in 1947/48, it was an excellent effort. This action shot shows to good effect the completely uncluttered lines of the bodyshell, the result of contemporary obsession among designers with streamlining.

One of the earliest of roughly forty-nine 356s built at Gmünd, Austria, sits in front of the mid-engined prototype, 1948. The Gmünd-built cars were almost entirely made by hand, and differed most markedly from the later Stuttgart-built production cars in having alloy instead of steel bodyshells. The 356's air-cooled, rear-mounted, 1086cc, twin-carburettor engine developed just 40bhp, but due to lightweight construction a top speed of 80mph was easily on the cards. In this shot, visible Beetle-sourced components include the headlamps, 16-in five-stud wheels and sickle-shaped bumper overriders.

A cabriolet version of the 356 featured from the earliest days of Gmünd production. The majority of cabriolet bodies were constructed by Beutler in Switzerland, while a handful were built by Austro-Tatra in Vienna, and by the Keibl coachbuilding concern. Each example was individually made on chassis supplied by Porsche, and differed in detail from one to the next. Unlike the coupe in the last photograph, this cabriolet has 'clap-hands' windscreen wipers, polished aluminium hubcaps and considerably less body 'overhang'. Regrettably, few of these cars survive.

Automotive engineers have something of a reputation for being quiet, industrious, patient types. However, they are rarely happy about the huge workload imposed as a result of having to convert perfectly good left-hand-drive cars to right-hand drive for the benefit of people in countries like Britain who insist on driving on the 'wrong' side of the road. This 1951 cabriolet is the first right-hooker to be exported to Australia. The first right-hand-drive exports to Britain also began in 1951. Note the central position of the single exhaust tail-pipe.

Nowadays, many owners of valuable classics like the 356 are proud of their gleaming steeds, and spend countless hours polishing them to a beautiful mirror finish. This archive picture illustrates perfectly what Porsche ownership in the 1950s was actually about. This Gmünd competition coupe has dull, travel-stained paintwork, and the bottom of the door and sill are bent, but Porsches were built for hard driving. Battle scars were almost inevitable but rarely detracted from the important business of getting a move on.

Ferry Porsche had modestly envisaged that 356 production would be limited to a maximum of 500 units. Happily for the future of the company, this prediction was one of very few that he got horribly wrong. Shot in 1953, this official publicity photograph of a coupe is interesting for its use of an elegantly clothed model. This was not only designed to catch the attention of men, but makes the point that women also owned and drove exciting sports cars, including Porsches, during the 1950s.

It is a great pity that so few professional photographers bother with overhead views, because these often show off a car's body lines better than the more normal lens angles. Particularly distinctive in this illustration of the four-seater prototype is the 'bent' windscreen, a feature of all 356s until the advent of the 356A in 1955.

From this 'head-on' view the four-seater is indistinguishable from the regular coupe, but the contrast between sunlight and shade illustrates the aesthetic appeal of the 356 to extremely good effect. With apparent styling influence from the Volkswagen Beetle, the Porsche's curves are deeply rounded, and in contrast to contemporary British and Italian sports machines, the Porsche is inevitably without a chromed radiator grille to interrupt airflow over the sheet metal.

The Porsche factory at Zuffenhausen where assembled and unfinished coupes predominate, 1952. However, there are two real Porsche rarities in the foreground (left) and middleground (right). These are America Roadsters (Type 540) with bodies built by Heuer in 1952. Intended primarily for the American market, these open-top cars had distinctive 'hump-back' styling and, devoid of superfluous trim and equipment, were intended for competition purposes. Unfortunately, Heuer closed its doors in late 1952 and Roadster production was abruptly halted after sixteen cars had been completed.

America Roadsters had 'cut-down' doors, a rudimentary soft-top, leather bonnet straps, aluminium seats and a detachable windscreen. For racing purposes the bumpers and hubcaps were also removed. Having shed up to 115lb of unnecessary bits and pieces, these agile cars had a power-to-weight ratio superior to contemporary Ferraris and Jaguars. Fitted with the 1500cc pushrod engine, the top speed of the Roadster was about 95mph, but those skinny 16-in crossply tyres necessarily limited cornering adhesion.

Jack McAfee at the wheel of his Roadster at the Moffett Field, USA, race track, 1953. Weight-saving measures on this example have even been extended to removal of the Porsche badge, indicators and bonnet handle, and the regular windscreen has been changed for a Perspex deflector. Resembling an inverted chamber pot, the driver's crash helmet is typical of the period, and as much use for its intended purpose as a fire extinguisher in an active volcano.

Motor-sport enthusiast, Heinrich Sauter, built this delectable Roadster in 1951 for his own personal use. Remarkably, it weighed some 115kg less than Porsche's America Roadster but, despite its obvious potential, Sauter campaigned it throughout 1951 in minor sports-car events without success. At the end of the season he lost interest in the car and sold it to Frenchman François Picard, who painted it blue and raced it as the 'Petit Tank'. Note that this car has two separate aero screens.

In 1953 the Sauter 'Petit Tank' turned up in the USA, and is seen here being fettled in the paddock prior to an event. The Jaguar XK120 coupe, MG TD and Sauter-Porsche would have created a great deal of interest for spectators at this time. Today, there is as much affection among Volkswagen fans for the wonderful Kombi Transporter service vehicle. Universally known as 'Barn-doors' after their massive, top-hinged engine lid, pre-1955 Volkswagen Transporters are much sought after, and have become collectors' pieces in their own right.

A cheerful snapshot of an America Roadster in the grounds of the Heuer factory, 1952. The photographer failed to get all his subjects looking into the lens but, in the tradition of so many amateurs, he too appears in the picture – he is clearly reflected in the paintwork behind the front wheel! Unfortunately, car manufacturers, forever operating under the watchful eye of their swish public relations gurus, just do not allow pictures of this nature to escape into the public domain nowadays. Dressed in their best vests, an official photograph of Porsche's current workers, dutifully lined up behind a Boxster, would not quite fit the company's image . . .

The 1951 Le Mans 24 Hours marked Porsche's first official venture into top-flight motorsport. Fitted with wind-cheating wheel spats, this 1.1-litre, alloy-bodied Gmünd coupe, driven by Veuillet/Mouche, ran like clockwork throughout. The car (now on display in the company's museum) not only won its class, and placed twentieth overall, it completed 1,777.665 miles at an average speed of 74mph, many laps having been completed at an average of 87mph. This success brought international recognition to Porsche, but it would be another nineteen years before the company would claim outright victory at the Sarthe.

Spiritual successor to the America Roadster, the 356 Speedster made its public debut in 1954. This model – a restyled and more austere version of the cabriolet – was built at the suggestion of American-based car importer Max Hoffmann. With its flimsy hood, shortened windscreen and sidescreens, in place of 'wind-up' windows, the car was especially popular in California both on and off the track. This early prototype shows the inverted 'bathtub' styling to particularly good effect.

Speedsters were available with the usual and bewildering variety of engines – 1300, 1500 and, from 1955, the 1600 – with either plain- or roller-bearing crankshafts. In addition to the pushrod engined cars there were also 1500cc, four-cam versions, primarily intended for racing, and a special GT variant with alloy doors and lids to further save weight. Note the 'humped' instrument binnacle and two-spoke steering wheel.

An official and evocative publicity shot of a 356A Speedster in Californian desert terrain, 1956. Unusually, the soft-top is in place, giving the car an awkward stance but welcome protection from potentially fierce sunshine. For tall folks the short windscreen was something of a nuisance, as the top of the frame naturally obscured vision. This necessitated having to sit very low in the seat, or peering over the top of the frame, which was impossible with the hood in position. Despite this inconvenience, Porsche found more than 4,800 enthusiastic customers for these desirable cars.

By contrast with the Speedster the regular cabriolet was a much more sensible car for everyday road use. Although its body was greatly reinforced, and heavier than the coupe, it was considerably more refined than the Speedster, and better protected against the elements with a more substantial soft-top. After the 'A' version, with its curved, panoramic windscreen, was introduced in 1955, the enlarged 1600cc engine also endowed the cabriolet with a reasonable turn of speed.

Speedsters were also available with a hard-top, supplied as an extra-cost option, but despite their practical value, many considered that they detracted from the car's out-and-out sporting aesthetics and purpose. The wire wheels, or *Speichenrader* in German, are 'after-market' items fitted by Walter Glöckler, the German motor-racing enthusiast whose home-built specials, constructed in the early 1950s, gave rise to the Porsche 550 sports racers in 1953.

Mid-1950s glamour in which the Speedster appears to be an incidental part of the composition. Photographs of this nature are fascinating for their innocence, charm and total lack of pretence. The car is obscured by a pretty girl feeding grass to an inflatable swan, an idea that certainly would not get past modern advertising people. Nowadays, automotive publicity has to be clever, sophisticated and capable of selling more and more cars – just one reason why more and more people are buying bicycles!

A German hillclimb event in which a Speedster is captured flat out kicking up dust, *c.* 1957. As is clear the road surface is extremely rough and loose, terrain on which Porsches excelled. With first-rate traction due to the rear weight bias, and robust construction in conjunction with completely unbreakable torsion-bar suspension, many Porsches won events like this purely because of their ability to remain in one piece.

The delectable 1500cc four-cam Carrera version was available from 1955. At first there were only coupe Carreras – a Speedster appeared slightly later – and two states of tune. The de luxe developed 100bhp at 6,200rpm, while the GT version pushed out 110bhp at 6,400rpm. These cars demanded to be driven really hard but, because they were extremely noisy inside the cabin, proved to be less popular among Porsche people than had originally been hoped. The 1.6-litre cars were dropped from the range in 1959, but a 2-litre Carrera reappeared in 1962 as an altogether more civilised car. Developing 130bhp at 6,200rpm, the Carrera 2 was capable of about 125mph, and was in every sense a real driver's car.

In American track events the Speedster in particular was a favourite mount with well-heeled club racers, for it was light, fast and naturally reliable. Triumph Roadsters, MGAs and Jaguars provided staple competition, the Jaguar's superior horsepower usually leaving the Porsches in the background but, for devotees of Zuffenhausen's products, the Speedster was without rival.

By contrast with the quick Carrera this Normal 356A coupe was fitted with the plain bearing 1.6-litre pushrod engine. With twin Solex 40 PICB carburettors and a compression ratio of just 7.5:1, it developed a comparatively modest 60bhp at 4,500rpm, sufficient for lively acceleration and a top speed in the region of 100mph. To many the pretty 356A was the classic 1950s roadgoing Porsche, for it had none of the 'bugs' of the pre-1955 cars, and was more attractive than the heavy looking 356Bs launched in 1959.

Happy days, which, regrettably, have long since gone. This is the works 356A Carrera of Strahle/Linge competing in the very last Mille Miglia in Italy, 1957. As its title inevitably suggests, the Mille Miglia was a 1,000-mile road race, and one of the most arduous and prestigious of its day. Unfortunately, the event had claimed the lives of both competitors and spectators; after de Portago's fatal crash on the 1957 outing, the Italian authorities wrapped it up for good.

Another relatively rare animal, a 356A four-cam Carrera with a hard-top. The idea behind this interesting exercise was to offer customers the best performance in a cabriolet that doubled as a usable 'tin-top' in inclement weather. The result is a thoroughly practical, high-speed sporting carriage, but one that was not especially popular. In styling terms the hard-top compromised the pretty shape of the coupe; it was not so much as an 'add-on' accessory, but something of a 'plonk-and-make-do' piece, which collectors today tend to store – permanently – on the walls of their garages.

The best of both worlds; a Speedster for her and, the purist's choice, a coupe for him. Taken in 1956 this wonderful publicity picture seeks to portray something of a glossy, romantic view of Porsche ownership. The important background to this picture, however, was not the large house and expertly landscaped gardens, but the Suez crisis, which led to serious fuel shortages and rationing in several European countries. Suez was the political conflict that nearly brought BMW to its financial knees but, happily, Porsche rode the storm extremely well.

Porsche's design consultancy work led to a number of commissions from various sources. This 1953 Studebaker (Porsche Type 542), pictured outside the Solitude Castle near Stuttgart, admirably illustrates Zuffenhausen's understanding of 1950s American thinking. With its water-cooled, front-mounted engine, huge boot, spacious four-door cabin and vast tracts of undistinguished sheet metal, the car is the antithesis of Porsche philosophy.

Two versions on the same Porsche Type 542 theme for Studebaker, a two-door coupe (right) rubbing shoulders with the four-door saloon. Both are unmistakably in keeping with the worst excesses of Detroit and, to European eyes, downright ugly. This aside there's little disguising the 356's influence in the bonnet and headlamps of the four-door saloon.

A multi-purpose vehicle, the Jagdwagen (Porsche Type 597), with switchable four-wheel drive, was built in the 1950s, and intended for use by the West German Army. Powered by a 1.6-litre 50bhp Porsche engine, and largely based on the wartime Porsche-designed Volkswagen Kübelwagen, prototypes acquitted themselves especially well in testing. The vehicle was the result of a competition among German designers, the Department of Defence Engineering and Procurement having put the project out to tender. Here, Porsche's competition manager and chief press officer Huschke von Hanstein is seen at the wheel during preliminary trials.

Like the Beetle, the Jagdwagen was so well made that it was capable of floating on water. However, this cross-country vehicle failed to go into series production. The Army contract was awarded to Auto-Union who had built a DKW cross-country vehicle. In testing the Porsche had proved to be superior, but a senior member of the Auto-Union concern had let it be known to the authorities in Bonn that, without a contract to supply DKWs to the Army there would be mass redundancies at the Auto-Union factory in Ingolstadt. The Jagdwagen had been an expensive risk, of which Ferry Porsche commented: 'From this point on I made up my mind never to lift a finger in this section again unless there was a firm order on the table. This was a decision I was to stick to in future.'

The automotive equivalent of Moussorgsky's piece *Pictures at an Exhibition*, Porsche's Type 534 came into existence for so many to wonder why. This was a project for Volkswagen, shown to the Wolfsburg concern's chief executive Heinz Nordhoff in late 1953. This prototype was constructed on a short wheelbase and bore resemblance to the 356, but failed to go into production. It held no advantages over the Beetle or Porsche 356, and wound up being used for technical research purposes.

In profile the Type 534 more closely resmbles a production 356 and, of course, there are undertones of the Beetle's styling. Like so many cars from this period this prototype coupe sits at an akwardly gawky ride height, with wheels and tyres that would look more at home on a pedal-powered kart. It is not difficult to imagine, though, that Volkswagen's history might have been very different if the car had been presented to Nordhoff with much lowered suspension and a slinky set of sports wheels.

Another project for Volkswagen, the Type 726/2 of 1953 was intended as a potential replacement for the Beetle. Naturally, the engine was in the rear and air-cooled, but the 'full-width', self-supporting body was to a much more conventional design. Of all the prototype work undertaken by Porsche for Volkswagen, this car arguably bears the closest resemblance to the VW Type 3 saloon that went into production in 1961.

Work on this Type 675 was carried out for Volkswagen between 1955 and 1959. Intended as a small two-door coupe it had a number of different power units fitted for experimental purposes. They included 1.2- and 1.5-litre V6 engines developing 43bhp and 54bhp respectively. There were also three-cylinder and two-cylinder engines, inspired by Fiat's talent for producing small, light cars with economical power units, but, alas, Volkswagen correctly predicted that its future lay with development of the Beetle.

Closely related to its sisters the 726/1 fastback and 726/2 notchback, this short-wheelbase Type 728 prototype was built by Porsche in 1960. Sporting an air-cooled, four-cylinder 'boxer' engine this was yet another attempt at a car ultimately aimed at replacing the venerable, aged Beetle. The roof section and window glass area are so obviously Beetle-inspired, but it made no impression on Heinz Nordhoff, who politely asked Porsche to think . . . yet again.

As Porsche's development work for Volkswagen evolved, further prototypes were built. On the right is the 728 – rejected by Heinz Nordhoff – with the Type 3 notchback (left) and fastback (centre). Pictured in 1958, the notchback and saloon are, more or less, in their definitive form, although the fastback did not go into series production until 1965. With their 1.5- and later 1.6-litre engines the Type 3s were quicker and more powerful than the 1200 Beetle, and there was much more cabin space but, by Volkswagen's standards these cars were failures. The Beetle's success lay largely in its unique styling, and loyal customers all over the world kept faith with the iconic insect for many years.

Apart from the company's experimental work and engineering commisssions from around the world, Porsche maintained development of the staple 356 model throughout the 1950s. The coupe, cabriolet and Speedster sold almost, but not quite, beyond Ferry Porsche's imagination but, by 1958, the Speedster had just about had its day. The market for a lightweight sports car devoid of 'fancy frills' was shrinking. Customers loved the shape of the Speedster, and all it stood for, but called for a few creature comforts.

To answer critics of the Speedster, Porsche introduced the Convertible D (D for coachmakers Drauz), which had a 'full-height' windscreen, 'wind-up' side windows and conventional seats in place of the sports-style 'buckets' fitted to the Speedster. Having made this new model Porsche then received flak from Speedster lovers – there's no pleasing some folk – and promptly introduced a Roadster version, devoid of most 'frills'.

In 1959 the 356A was superseded by the 356B, a 'facelifted' model with bigger bumpers, recontoured front wings and bonnet, and the headlamps mounted a little higher. In addition to the 1600 engines, which remained available in 60bhp and 75bhp guises, there was the new 90bhp Super 90 model. This also had a 1.6-litre engine but with a high 9.5:1 compression ratio, increased valve diameters and a brace of Solex P11-4 carburettors. With a top speed in the region of 110mph the Super 90 remained competitive in the 1600cc class, even though it was heavier than the model it replaced.

A perfect picture of a 1959 356B cabriolet 1600, in a setting designed to appeal to aspirant Porsche owners. The expensive cabriolet version remained popular throughout 356 production, but the coupe outsold it in 1959 by a ratio of three to one. On

the introduction of the 356B, cabriolets found just 944 customers – 438 fewer than in 1958 – but this figure rose to a slightly more encouraging number of 1,617 in 1960.

Introduced in 1959 the spartan Roadster version, with Speedster body styling, proved as popular as ever. In 1960 Porsche sold no fewer than 1,529 of these gorgeous cars. Available with the 1600 pushrod engines – but not the four-cam Carrera – the bodies were made in Brussels by Anciens Etablissement d'Iteren Freres SA, the Belgian Porsche importers. Like previous incarnations the soft-top was without a headlining, but luxuries included a cigar lighter and map pockets in the interior door panels.

An archive picture with a truly international flavour. The 356B Roadster is captured 'somewhere in Africa' which, judging by the 'CD' plate on the car's rump, was owned by a diplomat. It is almost impossible to imagine what the impoverished indigenous people, whose traditional transport came down to a choice between Shanks's pony or perhaps a bicycle, thought of a fast, noisy and exciting sports car during the late 1950s, let alone now.

Formed in the 1950s, the enthusiastic Porsche Club of America line their cars up for a photo shoot at the Solitude racing circuit near Stuttgart, 1959. The vast majority of cars are brand-new 356B coupes, which their owners would have collected from the factory and shipped home, having enjoyed a holiday into the bargain. By the beginning of the 1960s North America had become Porsche's most important and lucrative export market, and this remains the case today, of course.

Hard-tops for the cabriolets from 1958 were usually made from glassfibre, and detachable to offer owners the best of both motoring worlds. In 1960 Porsche also introduced the Karmann-built hard-top with a fixed steel roof. It held no advantages over the regular coupe, except for its larger glass area, but not everyone approved of the car's aesthetics and this model was dropped from the range in 1962. Karmann built approximately 699 fixed hard-top versions; few survive.

A number of specialist companies throughout the world built their own versions of the Porsche 356. This handsome steel-bodied creation was the work of the long-established coachbuilders Beutler, who had worked closely with Porsche for many years. This 1960 car is a four-seater fitted with a 1600cc pushrod engine, but had limited appeal despite its extra carrying capacity. Porsche were established as manufacturers of sports cars; four-seaters were for people with families and responsibilities, all of which had nothing to do with the enjoyment of driving a serious sports car.

A 1950s oddity from Argentina with 'clap-hands' windscreen wipers, extremely tall bumper overriders, ghastly hubcaps and bright mouldings on the body flanks and lots of people reflected in the paintwork. A creation in Porsche lore that is probably best forgotten . . .

In addition to the Beutler version of the four-seater 356, Porsche built a four-seater 901 (later the 911) in 1960. This was the work of Butzi Porsche, but it got no further than prototype stage. The case for a production version was over-ruled by Ferry Porsche himself, who reminded his colleagues of the reasons for the company's existence and continuing success. Four-seaters were not proper Porsches, although the company would go on to produce the four-seater 928 in mid-1970s, which also proved Ferry's views to be correct!

In 1961 the 356B received its final facelift when its body styling was slightly altered yet again. This was known as the T6 version – the original 'B' body was the T5 – and is seen here in Roadster guise. Cars built at the factory were never fitted with wire wheels, these being 'after-market' items, which do nothing for the car aesthetically or intellectually. These quaint old things had featured on sports cars during the inter-war years and had no business on engineering sophisticates of the 1960s.

The final version of the 356 appeared in 1963 as the 356C. This model retained the body styling of the T6, introduced in 1961, and is seen here in cabriolet guise with a detachable hard-top. This model's most significant advantage over previous models were all-round, Ate-made disc brakes, and radial tyres as standard fitments. Among the regular cars there were two engine choices, namely the 75bhp 'C' and 95bhp 'SC', both of which were 1.6-litre pushrod units. Note the twin air-intake grilles in the engine lid.

For Porsche fans on a big budget the 2-litre four-cam Carrera 2 was available from 1962, a purposeful piece of machinery developing 130bhp at 6,200rpm. Twin Solex 40 P11-4 carburettors, with their gauze-covered air filters, take up much of the engine compartment. A formidable and truly wonderful road car, the Carrera 2 was capable of well in excess of 120mph, and accomplishing the benchmark 0–60mph dash in 9.7 seconds. By comparison with today's cars – the 2-litre Porsche 924 has comparable performance – the Carrera 2 appears to be somewhat tame, but it is always worth recalling that an average family saloon from, for example, Ford in the early 1960s, began to run seriously out of steam at 60mph.

The 356C took its final bow in 1965 – a handful were also built in 1966 – to make way for the much more sophisticated six-cylinder 911. By comparison with so many contemporary sports cars, the 356 enjoyed a long innings having been officially in production for fifteen years. By the 1970s these classic Porsches had been all but forgotten, except by a minority of dyed-in-the-wool enthusiasts, and exchanged hands, often in poor condition, for laughably small quantities of cash. Thanks to people like Tony Dron, erstwhile editor of the British journal *Classic Cars*, old Porsches are now appreciated for what they are – finely made sports cars from one of the world's greatest manufacturers.

Chapter 2

FROM BEETLES TO SPYDERS – SPORTS RACING CARS, 1950–65

The car seen here is one of Glöckler's earliest cars; built in 1951 as a coupe with a 'quick-release' roof panel, it was fitted with an 85bhp version of the 1.5-litre Porsche pushrod engine. Sporting a Porsche badge on the front lid, these cars became known as Porsches in the German national press. During the late 1940s there was actually little difference between Beetle and Porsche parts, which is why the Müller and early Glöckler specials had similar performance.

Introduction

Although Germans were unable to take part in international motorsport until the early 1950s, a number of low-key events were held from 1948 when this war-torn country began to return to something approaching normality. While the great pre-war cars from Mercedes-Benz and Auto-Union would lie forever dormant, a number of private enthusiasts began to dust off their old saloons and sports cars. A handful of racing people, however, took a different route and built specials in the best tradition of skilled amateurs.

Among the most notable were Petermax Müller and Walter Glöckler, who constructed attractive alloy bodied open sports cars based on Volkswagen Beetle components. Glöckler was a Volkswagen dealer, fanatical about motorsport, and enjoyed great personal success with his lightweight, home-built job. However, by 1950 he had established a good relationship with Porsche and was able to build a new car fitted with an 85bhp, 1.5-litre Porsche engine.

With this car he set new speed records for 1500cc sports cars before selling it to Max Hoffmann in the USA, where it enjoyed some success in 'clubbie' events. This resulted in the construction of another Glöckler special – dubbed a Glöckler-Porsche – over the winter of 1951. Unlike the previous cars this version was based on a 356 chassis with its engine slung out in the tail, and had a coupe body with a detachable roof. The car bore more than a passing resemblance to the Porsche 356, was instantly successful and eventually went to Max Hoffman.

A further two Glöckler-Porsches were built and campaigned throughout the German national series in 1953, again with success, and became widely known, not as Glöckler 'specials' but as Porsches. The victories scored by Glöckler and his team considerably enhanced Porsche's reputation and sales of the 356 road cars, and by 1952 were beginning to cause Ferry Porsche to endure pangs of anxiety.

Ferry, more than anyone else in the company, was cognisant of the need to go motor racing on a bigger scale than had been accomplished with the diminutive 1.1-litre Gmünd-built 356s. Ferry also knew of the huge financial benefits to be gained from a successful motor-racing programme but, like his father before him, was ever mindful of the need for prudent housekeeping. On the other hand, Italian cars, along with Borgward and EMW from East Germany, had started to dominate the 1500cc class in European sports-car racing and this, naturally, put Porsche's future reputation at stake.

One of Porsche's key people, Baron Huschke von Hanstein, who was also in charge of the company's press relations, was largely responsible for persuading Ferry Porsche that a sports racing car was required – and urgently. Ferry relented and during 1952 the first Type 550 prototypes were built, largely along the lines of Walter Glöckler's earlier mid-engined specials.

A simple ladder-frame chassis, with six crossmembers, carried the ubiquitous torsion-bar suspension front and rear, the latter having the radius arms leading from the back of the chassis to the hub/swing-axle assembly, rather than trailing from the production 356's arrangement ahead of the rear wheels. Apart from the ZF limited-slip differential and hydraulically operated clutch, the major mechanical components were from the standard 356 road cars.

The two-seater alloy bodies were made by Weidenhausen in Frankfurt, and designed to allow for open-top (later known as 'Spyders' at Max Hoffmann's request) and enclosed coupe versions – the latter being primarily intended for Le Mans. Initially, these cars were fitted with the 1500cc Super pushrod engine. In its maiden race at the Nürburgring at the end of May 1953, the first car (550-01) ran on alcohol fuel and produced close to 100bhp, a remarkable power output for any pushrod engine. Driven by Walter Glöckler's cousin Helm the car suffered a little trouble with its twin Solex carburettors, but duly recorded a victory.

In the interest of reliability for Le Mans the cars ran on normal petrol, had a reduced compression ratio and power was limited to just 78bhp. In coupe form this allowed for a top speed of 125mph down Mulsanne. Despite engine problems, Paul Frere and Richard von Frankenberg won the 1500 class; the Porsche 'steamroller' had truly begun, but more power was needed from the flat-four if the success was to continue. Enter the Fuhrmann-designed four-cam engine.

This remarkably complex engine ran for the first time in April 1953, and teething difficulties were ironed out over the ensuing three months. The same style chassis for the second series cars was retained, but there were suspension improvements and a new, more aero-dynamically efficient body from the fertile mind of Erwin Komenda. The car debuted in practice at the Nürburgring, but was not raced, and finished third in a hillclimb event a week later in the capable hands of veteran driver Hans Stuck.

Two cars were sent to the USA to participate in a variety of races, but were not successful until Hans Herrmann scored third overall and first in class in the 1954 Carrera event in Mexico. Driving entirely on his own, Herrmann averaged an astonishing 97.62mph on this occasion and, along with the Herrmann/ Linge class win in the 1954 Mille Miglia, set the ball rolling for further development at the factory.

During its gestation period the 550 was subjected to body and chassis refinements, various changes particularly being made to the bodies in a quest to improve aerodynamic drag. During the 1954 Le Mans 24 Hours Porsche prepared a team of cars running with 1500 114bhp four-cam engines (and a 1.1-litre version), but a spate of piston failures made this outing something of a disaster. However, the Claes/Stasse Porsche salvaged Zuffenhausen honours with a class win and twelfth overall.

The 1954 1500 sports-car race at the Nürburgring, held on the same day as the German Grand Prix, was an important occasion for Porsche. Before the Second World War this event attracted much larger numbers of paying spectators than any motor-racing event in recent times, and victory here would provide the company with widespread, free publicity. Porsche got exactly what it had bargained for; the team of 550s romped home to fill the top four places, and further successes followed in the same year. By this time a number of cars were also being entered for sports-car races in the USA – the Porsche name was rapidly becoming well known, and the company's investment was beginning to pay handsome dividends.

Greater numbers of private customers began to take delivery of 550s, and used them for racing and hillclimbing and as fast road cars. Specifications differed, virtually to customer requirements, but few people ever got to grips with the car's road ability in the manner of regular drivers Richard von Frankenberg and Hans Herrmann. Although perfectly tractable under normal circumstances, the 550, like most cars predominantly built for racing, could be tricky at the limit – for those who ever found the limit. Some drivers complained of excessive oversteer, others of understeer, while Porsche quietly got on with preparing further cars for the great sports-car events.

A team was fielded for Le Mans 1955 with revised Wendler-made alloy bodies. With a top speed down Mulsanne close to 140mph, the cars were competitive and ran with Porsche's customary clockwork monotony. Richard von Frankenberg and Helmut Polensky drove a copybook race, bringing the first Porsche home in fourth place to score a class win and victory in the Index of Performance.

This triumph, though, was overshadowed by motor racing's worst-ever accident. In an an attempt to avoid running into the rear of Mike Hawthorn's Jaguar, Lance Macklin's Healey swerved into the path of Pierre Levegh's Mercedes 300SLR, which was immediately launched into the crowd opposite the pits. Levegh lost his life in the inferno, along with more than eighty spectators. In September of the same year the motoring world, and Porsche in particular, received more unwelcome publicity after the Hollywood film actor James Dean took delivery of a 550 Spyder and died in a high-speed accident on a California freeway.

By the mid-1950s Porsche's sports pro-gramme was gathering pace, and the people at the factory were confident of being able to make improvements as a result of lessons learnt, particularly at Le Mans. More than eighty 550s had been made between 1953 and 1956, with several falling into the hands of influential people like John von Neumann and Max Hoffmannn in the USA.

Further successes followed in 1956, but it had become clear to Porsche that a faster, improved car would soon be required. Quick, agile sports cars with relatively small capacity engines had become a Porsche speciality, but it was evident that there was stiff competition on the horizon from Lotus and Cooper, and there were always the Italians and their ever-present 'bloody red cars' to consider as well.

With a revised, much stiffer chassis frame, low-pivot swing-axle rear suspension and a reworked engine running with a higher 9.8:1 compression ratio and Weber, instead of Solex, carburettors, the 1956 550A RS (RennSport) cars were much easier to drive, and faster at the limit. Thanks to wider brake shoes they were also endowed with impressive anchor power, the equal of virtually all rivals.

It was with one of these cars that Porsche attempted to claim one of the world's biggest and best prizes in European road racing. Held over the rough, winding public 'tracks' of Sicily, and usually in fierce heat, the Targa Florio was an endurance race that tested drivers to the boundaries of bravery and foolhardiness, and cars to breaking point and beyond. Accidents were inevitable and usually spectacular, and the best survived through the most heightened and adrenalin-supported skill, and sheer luck.

For the 1956 event, held in June, Huschke von Hanstein teamed up with Italian Umberto Maglioli in what Porsche officially described as a private entry. The lone 550 Porsche actually had works backing, but on a laughably small scale. Naturally, the 3-litre Maseratis and 3.5-litre Ferraris were hotly tipped as the most likely winners, but the Targa made no distinction between engine sizes. It was unkind to all. By the second lap Maglioli took the little Porsche into the lead, the big boys having been delayed by serious mechanical failures, and 8 hours later scored the first of Porsche's eleven outright victories in this important event.

However, like all manufacturers, Porsche had its share of bad luck. In 1956 the company made a version of the 550 (the Type 645), which had a shorter wheelbase, narrower body and smaller frontal area in the interests of reducing drag. The car was a complete lemon, with unpredictable handling and an apt nickname, 'Mickey Mouse', – bestowed upon it by its only driver, Richard von Frankenberg.

Frankenberg raced the car at the Avus circuit near Berlin. This comprised two parallel stretches of autobahn joined by a hairpin at one end and a steeply banked curve paved with bricks at the other. The track had been the scene of titanic battles between the streamlined Mercedes and Auto-Unions before the Second World War, where these cars reached speeds in excess of 200mph. In view of the nature of the track – lethal in the wet – and the engine power and skinny tyres of the pre-war cars, it is little wonder that many of the people known to this author, who were lucky enough to have witnessed the Silver Arrows there, are often at pains to describe current Formula 1 events as sport for 'wimps'.

Richard von Frankenberg's outing in 'Mickey Mouse' ended abruptly when the car suddenly turned right on the banking and threw its driver on to an earth bank. Richard recovered from this ignominious event, but 'Mickey Mouse' at least had the good sense to comprehensively destroy itself. However, not even the worst cars are entirely useless, as they serve as bad examples to the rest. Porsche had learned a valuable lesson with this car for, despite its drawbacks, it paved the way for an improved RS Porsche.

This was the 718 RSK which, like its predecessor, utilised the 1500cc four-cam engine mounted amidships, and traditional torsion-bar rear suspension. The front suspension, however, radically broke with Porsche tradition: torsion bars were retained as the springing medium, of course, but were arranged, along with ball joints for steering control, in the shape of a letter 'K' (from which the car takes its name). With this arrangement Porsche were able to create a much lower bodyshell, with fared headlamps and a deeply curved nose panel to form a far more 'slippery' and faster car.

The RSK made its debut in practice for the Nürburgring race in 1957, the car's excellent performance giving confidence for what turned out to be an unsuccessful outing at Le Mans in June. Due to its light weight and low polar moment of inertia, though, the car was initially difficult to drive. Although its cornering speeds were very high – grip was phenomenal – loss of adhesion usually resulted in an uncontrollable spin. This was addressed over the winter of 1957; subtle alterations were made to the front suspension, and the rear was changed entirely for a Watts linkage, low-pivot driveshafts and coil springs. In one fell swoop this eliminated the extreme camber changes of the rear wheels and made the car entirely stable under hard cornering.

The RSK was the first of Porsche's 'sophisticates' – still a road-racing sports car that could be driven by amateurs, but one that was becoming increasingly deserving of the most skilled and gifted drivers. It proved to be successful in the hands of privateers and works' drivers on both sides of the Atlantic, a giant-killer that rocked established manufacturers like Ferrari, Jaguar and Aston Martin.

For the 1958 Le Mans 24 Hours Porsche fielded RSKs with 1.5- and 1.6-litre four-cam engines and caused embarrassment to a number of more powerful cars. Hans Herrmann and Jean Behra took third overall (winning the 2-litre class), and Edgar Barth and Paul Frere placed a 1.5-litre car in fourth overall to win the 1500 class. Second overall for the Behra/Scarlatti Porsche in the Targa Florio in the same year made so many seriously wonder what they had to do to stem the rising tide of the Stuttgart concern. It just was not normal for 1.5-litre cars to see off 3-litre Astons and Ferraris, but Porsche were proving that it could be done.

While Jaguar rested on its laurels, Ferrari and Porsche did not. Aston Martin came to the fore briefly in 1959 and scored the British concern's only win at Le Mans, but aristocratic bumbling would also see Aston's fortunes slip away over the ensuing years. Placing the engine in the middle of the chassis to improve roadholding was perpetuated by Porsche. Clever people like Charles Cooper and Colin Chapman were bright enough to realise that this was the way forward in car design. Mathematical principles were not to be denied, except by those who proved to be incapable of throwing off the shackles of tradition. These same people were of the opinion that racing drivers should wear tweed jackets for racing, fly home from an event in a Sopwith Camel bi-plane and celebrate success or failure with as many pints of beer as the system would take.

Ferry Porsche was gratified by his company's success in sports-car racing, but never lost sight of the reasons for indulging in this expensive sport. Racing was for the purpose of selling cars and improving engineering techniques. In his autobiography *Cars are My Life* (Patrick Stephens Ltd), he commented:

I am of the opinion that sports cars actually foreshadow innovations, and that this was true in the past as it will be in the future. Sports cars will never of course be produced in large numbers. It is logical therefore to use them to implement and test new ideas before they are put into series production. Being a lover of sports cars, that is of fast two-seater cars, has nothing to do with the fact that these cars have a top speed of 125 or even 180mph (200 or 290 km/h). The top speed is actually the result of mechanical efficiency and air resistance, and is thus a merely automatic process. It is not of course necessary to drive at these high speeds, but it is possible if one wants to, and that is probably the reason why many people consider sports cars to be unnecessary.

Throughout 1959 and 1960 the RSKs were hugely successful in all sorts of championships around the world, and naturally Porsche continued to develop the car. In 1959 the rear suspension was revised for a second time, the Watts linkage system being replaced by upper and lower wishbones and coil springs.

After Jean Behra converted his private RSK into a single-seater Formula 2 car, Porsche were inspired to build their own versions, and then went on to Formula 1 for 1961. As a result the sports-car programme suffered a little, but this single-seater flirtation was not successful, and the company quickly reverted to its original speciality.

For the 1960 season motorsport's governing body, the FIA, rewrote regulations governing sports cars. The most controversial of the new rules compelled manufacturers to increase windscreen height to a minimum of 25 cm, an aerodynamic burden to the little Porsches. Porsche complied, despite initial protests, and the result was the RS60 – an RSK with a 'full' windscreen. Maserati, on the other hand, openly flouted the new rules. Their 'birdcage' model had a huge windscreen that complied with the regulations, but much of the glass area was positioned in the space previously occupied by the bodywork. This was outside the spirit of the rules, but perfectly legal.

Porsche's RS60 also had a wider cockpit than the 1959 RSK, again to comply with new regulations, and the wheelbase was lengthened with a view to improving the car's stability out of fast corners. Needless to say, the RS60 proved to be as successful as its predecessors. Jo Bonnier and Graham Hill scored a convincing win in the Targa Florio (Porsche's second successive victory in this event) with the Gendebien/Herrmann Porsche in third place behind a 3-litre Ferrari.

After this race Denis Jenkinson and Jesse Alexander took a works Carrera 356 out on the circuit for a fun drive. Naturally, they had the time of their lives but, as 'Jenks' commented, they ran into a spot of bother. He remarked: 'On the way back to Cefalu, Jesse unfortunately hit a stray dog. Luckily it did no more damage than to break a sidelamp glass, but von Hanstein was quick to point out that he and Pucci had driven the car for 14 laps of the Targa Florio circuit without so much as putting a scratch on it. Now two journalists had smashed the sidelamp while out on a joy-ride. We had no answer to that.'

Sporting a 1,679cc engine Bonnier and Olivier Gendebien finished second at the Nürburgring, but Le Mans would be Ferrari's for the following five years. In 1960 the red cars, except for the third-place Aston Martin of Jim Clark and Roy Salvadori, filled the first six places, Linge/Walter bringing the Porsche home in tenth place for a class victory. There was, however, overall victory for Porsche in the 1960 European Mountain Championship.

Despite the high purchase price of these Porsches, privateers bought them in increasing numbers and for a variety of purposes. Competitive, fast, fun and relatively easy to maintain, apart from the ignition and valve timing, which was of potentially nightmarish proportions, they were also relatively easy to drive. An amateur could shine in a Porsche, and even win.

For 1961 Porsche continued with the same car, but now known as the RS61. Variations included long-wheelbase cars, intended to run with a revised version of the eight-cylinder Grand Prix car's power unit, and enclosed coupes with wedge-shaped nosecones and larger headlamp covers. The first cars were completed in time for the Le Mans test weekend in April 1961, where the luxury of an enclosed cockpit found favour with the drivers. Porsche also tested disc brakes for the first time on this occasion, but these were not fitted to the race cars for the 24-hour race in June as it was felt that they lacked development.

For the 1961 Targa Florio, Porsche's principal entrants were RS60s of the previous year, the leading car driven by Stirling Moss and Graham Hill retiring just 4 miles from the finishing line while in the lead. However, a W-RS (a one-off, open-top version of the Le Mans coupe) rescued Porsche's honours by finishing second behind the winning Ferrari. Porsche's Le Mans outing in June was one of those occasions that all teams experience from time to time. Despite careful preparation, almost everything that could go wrong did go wrong, and Porsche returned to Zuffenhausen in something of a dejected fluster.

By this time the factory cars were running with 1.6-, 1.7- and 2-litre, four-cam engines, while work also went ahead on the W-RS open-top car fitted with a 2-litre version of the eight-cylinder Grand Prix car engine. The latter enjoyed a mixed bag of fortune in 1962; there were appearances on both sides of the Atlantic, and outings in the European Mountain Championship, but big prizes proved to be elusive. It appeared that the company's sporting activities were beginning to fall apart. However, they were not.

Porsche were merely part way through a steep learning curve and, in attempting to push the boundaries, had overstepped the limit. After shelving the Grand Prix programme, normality was restored, the 1963 Targa Florio providing firm evidence that the people at Zuffenhausen knew exactly what they were doing. Fitted with the 200bhp-plus, 2-litre, eight-cylinder engine, a 718 coupe, driven by Jo Bonnier and Carlo Abate, scored a convincing Targa victory despite suffering dire problems with the gearbox. Although Mike Parkes put up the fastest lap at an average speed of 66.83mph, Bonnier's average for the race was an astonishing 64.57mph – a new record at that time.

Porsche's challenge at Le Mans in 1963, however, again ended in failure, although a W-RS did managed to rescue eighth place, and the great Edgar Barth won the European Hillclimb Championship in 1963 in the W-RS. But Porsche needed a new car and a new direction. From 1964 it had both.

Work began on the Carrera GTS, or 904, in 1963. The creation of Ferry Porsche's eldest son Butzi, the car was designed and built in an exceedingly short period, and represented a departure from the company's traditional thinking. Inspired by Colin Chapman's example at Lotus, the 904 was Porsche's first sports car with glassfibre bodywork, a relatively new material in the motor industry that substantially reduced weight. Butzi's penmanship also ensured that the new two-seater coupe was not only purposeful, with a commendably low frontal area and effective wind-cheating ability, but was also extremely good looking. At the front there was evidence of influence from the W-RS, with long headlamp covers and shovel nose but, with its long tapered coupe back and Kamm tail, the body styling was very much in keeping with contemporary trends.

The chassis was also 'new' and novel. In place of the predominantly 'spaceframe' arrangement of the RSK series of cars, Porsche produced a steel girder-frame chassis with crossmembers. The two parallel girders ran from the front to the rear suspension units, and were reminiscent of the layout of the pre-war Auto-Union Grand Prix cars. Despite its light weight the frame was torsionally very stiff, and extremely rigid once the glassfibre body panels had been bonded directly to it. By comparison with the later specframes used for the 906 and subsequent models, the 904's chassis appeared to be crude and old-fashioned. Front and rear suspension was by wishbones and integral coil spring/damper units, this arrangement being virtually *de rigeur* in contemporary sports-car design. Braking was by all-round discs, virtually to the same specification as the standard 356 road car, and the wheels were the ubiquitous five-bolt items with steel centres and alloy rims. At just 5.5J and shod with 165 × 15 radial tyres the wheel rims and tyres were quaintly narrow.

Performance was reliant on the 2-litre version of the trusty four-cam unit, and private customers were eager to take delivery of the new cars, which were available from January 1964. Dramatic in appearance, and enormously rewarding to drive, the 904 was the last genuine sports GT car from Porsche that could be conducted to and from an event on public roads.

The car was also successful in a wide variety of events, Eugen Böhringer and Rolf Wütherich placing a works car in second overall in, of all events, the Monte-Carlo Rally. In his book *Porsche Past and Present*, Denis Jenkinson commented:

Some years afterwards, I was staying at Böhringer's hotel, which overlooks the Daimler-Benz factory in Unterturkheim, high up in the hills where the best German wines come from. On the wall of the restaurant is a photograph of that Monte Carlo 904 and when I remarked on it Böhringer chuckled and reminisced about the event. His lasting impression was of the coldness of the cockpit in mid-winter, for the heating system was negligible, and with the air-cooled engine behind him and no water radiator at the front he had virtually no protection from the cold. It was only a continual supply of brandy that kept him and his co-driver from freezing to death. He reckoned it was a riot of fun and something nice to have done, but 'never again'.

However, this is jumping the gun. Throughout 1964 the 904 carried Porsche's flag in a number of world-class events. With a maximum speed of 160mph, these agile little 2-litre cars were fast, but far from able to rub shoulders with 'top-flight' Ferraris. This aside, the car scored a class win on its debut at Daytona in February 1964. For the Targa Florio, held in April, Porsches once more excelled, the 904s of Davis/Pucci and Linge/Balzarini finishing in first and second. It was a convincing demonstration, which some declared to be a hollow victory in the absence of Ferrari.

At Le Mans there were five 904s entered and they finished in seventh, eighth, tenth, eleventh and twelfth places, which, if nothing else on this occasion, proved Porsche's long-distance reliability beyond reasonable doubt. Throughout 1965 904s were used extensively, and although competition from Ferrari in the 2-litre class was wanting, the Porsches once again proved to be successful.

The 1965 Le Mans 24 Hours car race was the last occasion during the twentieth century that a Ferrari scored an outright victory in the great French race. Driven by Jochen Rindt and Masten Gregory, the 3-litre 250LM ran almost faultlessly, but the winning era of Enzo's pretty V12-engined cars was at an end. Ford duly served notice that it was truly fed up with Enzo Ferrari, and the American concern immediately increased the stakes in the sports-car world. Porsche's highest placing in 1965 was fifth overall, sufficient for a class win, but it had

become obvious by the mid-1960s that the people in Zuffenhausen could no longer be content competing in the 'lower formula'.

The European Hillclimb Championship was also Porsche's in 1965, an ugly Spyder version of the 904 showing everyone a clean pair of heels. However, when the regular works cars were fitted with the 2-litre, eight-cylinder and six-cylinder engines, the 904 evolved into a much more specialised machine. The four-cylinder cars developed roughly 180bhp and had a top speed of about 160mph; the eight-cylinder cars by contrast developed in excess of 220bhp and were capable of 175mph, which was in a sense getting well away from the concept of a road car for track use, or vice versa.

Since 1951 Porsche had competed with cars in the very finest sports-car tradition. Over many years development had increased to the point where by 1965 the 904 had become a racing car. It certainly was not a Grand Touring car, as its original badging had suggested. Although the 904 was perfectly road legal, the eight-cylinder versions in particular demanded to be piloted by professional drivers of the highest calibre.

When the 904 was replaced by the 906 in 1966, the idea of driving the latest Porsche sports racing car to an event, competing and driving home again afterwards was virtually out of the question. Developing 210bhp the six-cylinder 906 began Porsche's march to the top of the sports racing world. The 906 demanded drivers who were both physically and mentally fit, for it was an incomparably noisy, finely honed racing car which, at the limit, would frighten the pants off the amateurs of yesteryear. In the three years between the launch of the 906 and the advent of the 917 in 1969, Porsche power had increased in output by an additional 400bhp, which effectively ended the amateur driver's role in top-level sports-car racing once and for all.

One of the open-top Glöckler Porsches with which its owner/constructor won the 1952 German Sports Car Championship. This particular example was fitted with the 1.1-litre version of the Porsche flat-four; running on petrol it developed close to 50bhp, and about 60bhp on methanol. Beautifully made, the Glöcklers' strength lay in their light weight, superb, agile handling and, of course, reliability. A small number of these cars were raced in the USA, most notably by Max Hoffmann, where they enjoyed a mixed bag of fortunes.

This view of the 1952/53 Glöckler admirably illustrates the advanced shape of the streamlined bodyshell. The clean metalwork is only interrupted by the bonnet and door shutlines, and air-intake louvres in the rear panel. Attention to detail includes holes drilled in the 'ears' of the wheel-locking nuts to further reduce weight. Although Beetle-like in appearance, the headlamps are actually Ford Taunus items.

Walter Glöckler built two further cars in 1953, this dual-tone Roadster being one of them. It was fitted with a 1.5-litre Super engine and roller-bearing crankshaft, and appeared as an official exhibit on the Porsche stand at the Geneva Motor Show. The car was bought and raced by Hans Stanek, who campaigned it in a number of Swiss events, before selling it back to Walter Glöckler. The sister Glöckler was raced by Richard Trenkel, who used it to good effect to win the German Sports Car Championship for 1,100cc cars. Unusually sporting hubcaps, the car seen here is also fitted with Ford Taunus headlamps.

Inspired by Walter Glöckler's splendid example, work began on the official Porsche Type 550 prototypes in the spring of 1953. There was a ladder-type chassis frame, mid-mounted, 1500cc Super engine and a simple alloy body built by Weidenhausen in Frankfurt. The car was intended primarily for an assault on the Le Mans 24 Hours, but first appeared in competition at the Nürburgring in 1953. Driven by Helm Glöckler, it was pitted against strong opposition from EMW and Borgward, and despite a problem with the carburettors, secured a well-deserved maiden victory.

There was a class win at Le Mans, victory for Hans Herrmann in the Nürburgring race for 1.5-litre cars that followed and a class victory on the Carrera Panamericana in August 1953. With air louvres in the revised rear wings this car is seen against the New York skyline before being shipped to Mexico for the Panamericana, where it ran in coupe format. This dusty, high-speed, five-day thrash on rough public roads was one of the toughest and potentially most hazardous events of its day. Note that twin Bosch horns have been mounted on the front panel.

Substantial revisions were made to the 550s in 1953. Painted in a particularly uninspired shade of green, with equally dull wheels, this example has high, upswept rear wings and is devoid of engine-cooling louvres behind the doors. In place of a rudimentary air deflector there is a 'full-height' windscreen, and the nosecone had a much smaller rectangular opening for the oil cooler. The most significant development was, of course, the Fuhrmann-designed, 1.5-litre, four-cam engine which, depending on its state of tune, was capable of propelling the car to a top speed of between 125–40mph.

Fitted with a front 'bumper' this particular example, nicknamed 'Buckelwagen' after its 'humped' section behind the driver and passenger's head, was entered for the 1954 Mille Miglia. Driven by Hans Herrmann and Herbert Linge, the car left the start at Brescia at 3.51 a.m., as its racing number indicates, but the German pair were very lucky to get away with their lives, let alone reach the finish. At one juncture, close to the small town of Chieti, the Porsche approached a railway crossing at high speed; the barrier was down, and there was a train approaching. Neither the train nor the Porsche stood a chance of stopping, so Herrmann and Linge ducked under the barrier and held their breath. They got away with it, but it was a very close shave.

The 550 on display after the 1954 Mille Miglia, Herrmann and Linge finishing with a class win and sixth place overall. This archive picture clearly shows the high centre section behind the driver and passenger, designed to improve airflow over the sloping tail. So compact was the four-cam engine, that it is almost out of sight here. Note that the car is fitted with five-bolt wheels instead of the 'quick-release' type with a central spinner.

Photographed in 1991, Hans Herrmann with the 550 he took to a class win and third overall in the 1954 Carrera Panamericana. This was an extremely successful year for the 550s, both as works' efforts and in private hands, and really put Porsche on the racing map. Media interest in the cars was considerable, and more importantly from Porsche's point of view, it was free. By the end of 1954 the cars were officially known as RS Spyders, a name that would remain with the open-top, sports-racing Porsches for many years.

Forever attempting to cheat air pressure, this Perspex bubble was fitted for the 1955 event at Hockenheim. A number of other manufacturers experimented with this 'demon tweak' at about the same time. Drivers doubtless appreciated the protection the 'bubble' gave them against wind and rain, but such treatment not only looked ridiculous, but created uneven turbulence at the rear of the car. By the end of 1955 this was yet another motorsporting bubble that had broken.

In 1956, the last year of development for the 1.5-litre 550, Porsche's amazing success continued and culminated in a resounding outright victory in the Targa Florio. The winning car was driven by Umberto Maglioli at an average speed of 56.4mph over the 446.4-mile course. The Porsche's closest rivals on this occasion were from Ferrari and Maserati, sporting 3.9- and 4.5-litre V12 engines respectively. Zuffenhausen's efforts would result in ten further Porsche victories in this great road race before motorsport's then governing body, the CSI, finally brought it to an end in 1973.

Driven by Richard von Frankenberg, the Porsche Type 645 made its debut at Solitude in 1956, and provided a link between the 550s and later RSK Type 718. An experimental four-cam machine, it had a short wheelbase, pretty styling with an open cockpit and was appropriately nicknamed 'Mickey Mouse'. Richard von Frankenberg was its only driver, and was lucky to escape with his life after the car suddenly turned right on the banking at the Avus circuit, throwing its driver out on to an earth bank. This unexplained accident resulted in the car comprehensively destroying itself, which came as something of a relief to Richard von Frankenberg.

The 550's successor, the RSK, was an altogether neater and lower car. It is seen here on its first appearance, at practice for the Nürburgring race in 1957, driven by 1956 Targa Florio winner, Umberto Maglioli. There was also an unsuccessful outing at Le Mans in June. Early cars suffered from 'twitchy' handling, which eventually resulted in major changes to the rear suspension. Modifications to the 1.5-litre engine, including the fitment of large Weber 46 IDM-1 carburettors, resulted in 142bhp at 7,500rpm. An enlarged 1.6-litre engine appeared in 1958.

One of motor racing's greatest characters, Jean Behra, who had a fearsome reputation for his no-nonsense, 'hands-on' approach to everything life has to offer, is seen here at the start of the 1958 Mont Ventoux Hillclimb at the wheel of an RSK. Behra was not an 'ace' but was afraid of no one; at Riverside, California, in 1958 he took one of these cars to fourth overall in a major race that included Jaguar and Ferrari's most powerful cars. Behra would go on to make a single-seater version of the RSK, which he drove successfully in Formula 2 until he was killed in a Porsche at Avus in the 1959 Berlin Sports Grand Prix.

The beautiful RSK was also an astonishingly successful design. Pictured at Sebring, 1958, against the logo of another successful company, these cars continued Porsche's reputation as giant-killers. In a comprehensive display of performance and reliability, RSKs filled the top three places in the 1959 Targa Florio, the winning car of Barth/Seidel averaging an impressive 56.61mph over the 624.96-mile course. While Le Mans 1958 had been a success, with Porsches in third, fourth and fifth places, the 1959 French classic had been a disaster, with one car after another developing mechanical problems. But even Porsche are allowed to fail sometimes.

Arguably one of the prettiest Porsches, the 1959 RSK developed upwards of 155bhp, but was not especially easy to drive by comparison with the 550 series. The car was fast, but finely honed for its primary purpose of racing. Although the RSK was a road car, predominantly for traditional road racing, development and the quest for greater performance inevitably led to a situation in which the car demanded to be driven by the best drivers. As professionalism, inaugurated by Stirling Moss, began to creep into the sport, the gulf between amateurs and works' pilots began to develop quickly – and it showed.

Dutchman Carel de Beaufort, a loyal Porsche customer and driver for many years, with the 1959 Behra-inspired central-seater RSK. Something of a wild card in the cockpit, he formed his own racing team, Ecurie Maarsbergen, but although he eventually calmed down, his career in sports cars and Formula 1 was relatively undistinguished, and ended with a fatal crash in practice for the German Grand Prix in 1964. It is worth comparing de Beaufort's physique with that of modern drivers.

For 1960 the RSK was modified to include a 'full-height' windscreen and wider cockpit, and was dubbed the 718 RS60 Spyder. This example, driven by Ulrich Heyl, is competing in the 1989 Oldtimer Grand Prix at the Nürburgring. The tall windscreen, demanded by newly introduced regulations, was openly but legally flouted by Maserati; Porsche stuck to the letter of the law and paid an aerodynamic penalty in consequence. Porsche's revenge, however, was sweet, as Jo Bonnier and Graham Hill scored outright victory in the Targa Florio. The many 'experts' who claim that Graham Hill was devoid of natural driving talent may be right, but the fact remains that the Londoner is the only man in motor-racing history to have won the Formula 1 World Championship (twice), the Le Mans 24 Hours, the Indianapolis 500 and the Targa Florio.

The Porsche team entered for the June Le Mans comprises a trio of RS60s and one of the beautiful 356-based 1600 GS Carrera GTL Abarths. The drivers were: Barth/Seidel (39), Trintignant/Herrmann (34), Bonnier/Hill (33) and Linge/Walter (35). The outing was disastrous for the team, the first Porsche home finishing in a lowly eleventh place. Note that the cars were fitted with additional driving lamps for this event.

Truly beautiful Porsches, the four-cam Abarth Zagato Carreras had their alloy bodies fashioned in Turin. Porsche originally ordered twenty of these cars, the idea being to get a really light, slippery sports car with a small frontal area. The aim of low aerodynamic drag was admirably achieved, but at the expense of driver comfort. The cabin was cramped and the driving position truly Italian, but this did not prevent Paul Strahle and Herbert Linge scoring a maiden class victory and sixth overall in the 1960 Targa Florio. Note that the standard Porsche 356 taillamps are fitted, but positioned vertically.

The highest-placed Porsche finisher at Le Mans 1960, this Carrera GTL was driven by Linge and Walter to eleventh overall and class victory in the GT category. It was not an especially comfortable outing for the two Germans, though. The 1960 24 Hours was extremely wet, and the Abarth Carrera had a particular talent for taking water aboard. Its floorpan and seats were awash throughout, and although Linge and Walter wore skidlids and racing overalls, wetsuits and diving goggles might have been more appropriate.

Heini Walter's Swiss-registered RS60 at the start of the Freiburg Hillclimb, 1961. Regrettably, grand hillclimb venues are no longer a feature of the European sports-car championship, having simply died out in the 1960s. This is a great pity because this exacting branch of the sport not only tested drivers and machines, but gave spectators an opportunity to get really close to the track action. Despite the great beauty of the Porsche, the lady photographer on the right has obviously found something of greater interest.

Strictly speaking the 1961 Type 787 four-cylinder Grand Prix single-seater has no place in a volume about Porsche's road cars, but is included because it was clearly registered for road use. This was simply because in those happy, carefree days mechanics frequently drove the cars from the team's base – often several miles from a circuit – to the track, and back again at the end of the day. This was, of course, illegal but common sense prevailed. Porsche's race engineer Wilhelm Hild (with cigarette) is pictured here with Butzi Porsche; the latter has never made any secret of his dislike for wearing a tie. Note the DKW saloon in the background.

A brace of RS61s await despatch to Sicily for the Targa Florio, April 1961. On this occasion the Porsches had to play second fiddle to the 'bloody red car' of 'Taffy' von Trips (killed in a Ferrari at Monza in 1961) and Belgian Olivier Gendebien. The winning Ferrari covered the 446.4-mile course at an average speed of 64.27mph, with the Porsches of Jo Bonnier and Dan Gurney, and Hans Herrmann and Edgar Barth placing second and third respectively. Note that the car on the trailer (fitted with VW Transporter wheels and hubcaps) has rear mudflaps and a rear-view mirror mounted high on the windscreen.

In 1961 Porsche built a number of different cars, broadly along the RSK 718 theme. In readiness for the 1961 Le Mans 24 Hours the team comprised the prototype RS61 for Bonnier and Gurney (30, far right), the similar car for Barth and Herrmann (32), the Type 718 W-RS Spyder for Gregory and Holbert (33), and the 356 1600GS Carrera GTL Abarth for Linge and Pon (36). Ferrari 3-litres claimed the top three placings at the Sarthe on this occasion, and there was a 3-litre Maserati in fourth, but the Gregory/Holbert 2-litre, eight-cylinder W-RS rescued fifth place for Porsche, and the 1.6-litre Linge/Pon Carrera Abarth won its class and placed tenth overall. Ben Pon was the man who, in 1947, drew a simple pencil sketch of a Panelvan that led to the production of Volkswagen's Type 2 Transporter from 1950.

The 1962 version of the 718 GTR coupe looking a trifle forlorn on the rain-soaked tarmac of the Porsche factory prior to the 1962 Targa Florio. Painted red and fitted with a 210bhp version of the 2-litre, eight-cylinder engine, the car was capable of 160mph with ease, and finished third overall in the hands of Vaccarella and Bonnier. The 1962 Targa saw a Ferrari victory for the second year in succession, but Porsche would win in both 1963 and 1964. It was this car that would inspire Butzi Porsche's design for the later 904.

An open Spyder version of the eight-cylinder W-RS is photographed in bright sunshine prior to the 1963 Targa Florio. In the event it was a coupe version of this magnificent car, driven by Bonnier/Abate, that would claim overall victory. The Ferrari of Scarfiotti/Bandini/Mairesse placed second with the Barth/Linge Porsche in third.

One of the most glorious and perfect 2-litre sports cars of the 1960s, Porsche's 356B 2000 GS/GT was campaigned with the four-cylinder, four-cam unit in GT racing, and proved most successful. A perfectly proportioned sculpture in alloy, these powerful machines could easily top 140mph, and were joyful to drive, despite the total lack of aural protection from the large-bore exhaust system.

A 356B 2000 GS/GT on the famous banked Karussel at the Nürburgring, 1963. From this camera angle it is almost impossible to appreciate the daunting nature of this steep, high-speed corner, which has always had the capacity to unsteady the nerves of first-timers. In a sister car to this example, Edgar Barth and Herbert Linge won the 2-litre class and placed fourth overall in the Nürburgring 1,000km sports-car race, a proper 6-hour endurance event that is also missing from the annual calendar nowadays.

After the classic RS series cars Porsche launched the advanced and beautifully proportioned 904. Designed by Butzi Porsche, this was the company's first 'production' sports GT with fibreglass bodywork, and a girder-frame chassis. The vast majority of 904s were fitted with the four-cylinder, four-cam 2-litre engines, but six- and eight-cylinder versions were also campaigned in international sports-car racing. Typically, the four-cylinder cars developed in the region of 180bhp, and were capable of close to 160mph. Photographed in Stuttgart, 1963, this early test 'mule' appears to be unpainted. From this angle the 904 bears an uncanny resemblance to the Dino Ferrari 246 launched in 1968.

Badged as a Carrera GTS the 904 is put on public display at Wiesbaden, 1964, and is obviously causing a great deal of interest among those present. This was, all said and done, Germany's most exotic and exciting sports car at this time, and the last of the true GTs that could be driven on public roads. A styling masterwork, the 904, like all great classics, has body lines that have never dated. It is this author's guess that a 're-released' version of this car today would create an equal sensation to the original.

A travel-stained roadgoing version of the 904, quaintly fitted with chromed hubcaps, poses with skis for an official publicity photograph. That a mid-engined sports car with a complex four-cam engine could be used in snow and ice to transport its occupants to the ski slopes of the European alps and compete successfully in international motorsport was, of course, utterly ridiculous, but the role of a traditional sports car was ever thus. As Porsche's racing development galloped ahead in future years, the 911 would spiritually replace the 904 as the company's all-rounder.

The 904 competed in a huge variety of events throughout 1964, including Le Mans, where Ferrari were victorious once again. During this same year the Porsche's greatest hour came at the Targa Florio, where the standard roadgoing four-cylinder cars of Pucci/Davis and Balzarini/Linge placed first and second. The winning car's average speed – 62.16mph – for the event was slower than the Bonnier/Abate pace during the 1963 Sicilian classic, but was yet another demonstration of Porsche's talent for constructing relatively underpowered cars that went like stink.

Driven by Ben Pon and Gerhard Koch, this 904 is seen on the Nürburgring's Karussel, 1965. It is a glorious study of a well-balanced car at speed, midway through a notoriously difficult corner. Wonderful as the medium of colour photography is, a picture, no matter how good, cannot convey the unique, ear-splitting note of the four-cam engine, or the characteristic cackling and spitting of the exhaust system with the engine on over-run.

Eugen Böhringer and Rolf Wütherich took this 904 to a remarkable second place in the 1965 Monte-Carlo Rally. Outright victory might have been theirs had it not been for an unfortunate incident at a fuel stop. Böhringer pulled in for petrol and he was served by an enthusiastic pump attendant, who promptly dispensed lots and lots of fuel into . . . the Porsche's oil tank.

Böhringer's immaculate 904, fitted with additional driving lamps and twin Bosch horns on the front panel, was cleaned up prior to the prize-giving at the finish of the 1965 Monte. Böhringer reckoned the event to have been a lot of fun, but an experience that he would never want to repeat. The Monte-Carlo Rally in 1965 was held in cold, snowy conditions for much of its length, and the 904 was not equipped with a heater system. Böhringer and Wütherich depended on a regular top-up of brandy to sustain body and soul, a necessity then but one which would not be tolerated today.

The Davis/Mitter 904, fitted with the powerful eight-cylinder version of the four-cam engine, awaits its driver at the start of Le Mans, 1965. This event was won by Jochen Rindt and Masten Gregory in a Ferrari 250LM – the last time that Ferrari would be victorious at the Sarthe. At the start of the 1969 24 Hours, Jacky Ickx's protest would finally end the age-old practice of the drivers sprinting to their cars when the flag fell at 4 p.m. Ickx considered it to be dangerous, as many drivers would forego the use of seat belts in an attempt to make a good start. After the entire field had left the start in 1969, Ickx sauntered across to his Ford GT40, strapped himself in and slowly drove off. Exactly 24 hours later he crossed the finishing line in first place, less than 2 seconds ahead of Hans Herrmann in the Porsche 908, to record the closest finish in Le Mans history. Ickx, the greatest and best all-round racing driver – ever, would go on to score a further five victories at Le Mans, four of them in Porsches.

The Davis/Mitter 904 was fitted with the eight-cylinder engine for the 1965 Le Mans 24 Hours. Developing in the region of 220bhp, this particular example was timed down the Mulsanne straight at a breathtaking 175.2mph. It is most interesting to reflect that this was accomplished with a car that was NOT fitted with wings and the many other aerodynamic devices seen on modern sports cars with similar top speeds. Equally interesting in this archive picture is the Esso advertising board opposite the pits. The French slogan reads: 'Put a tiger in your engine'. In Britain this fuel company's slogan was changed to: 'Put a tiger in your tank'.

Günther Klass (21) and Udo Schütz (22) on the front row of the grid, with a brace of beautiful Abarths behind, at the start of the Norisring Race, 1965. In the mid-1960s the cars were still refreshingly devoid of advertising logos, but the many hoardings along the grandstand's façade seek to extol the virtues of Bosch sparking plugs, Martini drinks, Coca-Cola and, quaintly, the Nürnberger newspaper. As this heady decade progressed commercial sponsorship, especially from the tobacco industry, would become more and more important as the cost of race-car development spiralled forever upwards.

Widely considered to be among the ugliest sports cars ever made, a Spyder version of the 904 appeared in 1965. This was not a road car in the same sense as the 904 coupe, but as a hillclimber it was extremely effective. The lightweight, glassfibre body was minimal and rudimentary, and the diminutive 'flip-up' headlamps (required by competition regulations) made the car even less aesthetically pleasing. The 904 Spyders ran with both the six- and eight-cylinder engines; happily their like will never be seen again.

Gerhard Mitter, seen here after success on the Gaisberg Hillclimb in 1965, enjoyed a number of high placings with the 904/8. This particular example was nicknamed 'the kangaroo', and fitted with the eight-cylinder engine. The unidentified film reporter in the passenger seat has a facial expression clearly indicating that short Perspex windscreens do not do an especially effective job. Classic cars in the background include an Alfa, Beetle and BMW 700 coupe.

Nicknamed the 'Contergan Baby', this 2-litre six-cylinder version of the 904 Spyder had an even uglier body than the regular car's. Pictured in June 1965 at the start of the Rossfeld Hillclimb, Gerhard Mitter is once again at the wheel of a purpose-built racer, which is clearly road registered. Mitter won this event comprehensively, despite the German's dislike of the car's road manners; 'twitchy' in corners and nervous over bumps, the Spyder required the utmost in driver input and skill to keep it between the hedgerows. Note the proximity of spectators to the race track.

A stretch of very wet public road close to the Hockenheim racing circuit with Huschke von Hanstein, Porsche's competitions supremo, blasting the eight-cylinder Spyder, September 1965. Close to the end of its useful career at this time, the Spyder had been an interesting exercise in Porsche history, and a successful hillclimber. As much as anything else this car had been an experiment to create as lightweight a machine as possible within a relatively limited budget. The lessons learnt by Porsche's engineers and designers would be employed to extreme effect in future projects, as the company's rivals soon discovered to their considerable cost.

In 1966 the 904 was replaced by the 906, or Carrera 6 as it was popularly dubbed, seen here at Le Mans, 1966. Originally fitted with a 210bhp version of the 911's six-cylinder, 2-litre engine, this was an out-and-out purpose-built racer that, unlike its predecessor, was totally unsuited to everyday road use. It was amazingly quick, exceptionally noisy, of course, and demanded to be booted hard by people who really knew what they were doing. Naturally, this 2-litre car was not going to score outright victory against the 4.7-litre Fords and V12 P3/4 Ferraris at high-speed venues such as Le Mans, but the 906's superb handling brought Porsche yet another first place in the 1966 Targa Florio.

The great Rico Steinemann hard at work in a long-tailed version of the 2-litre 906 at Rheims, 1967. Rheims, in the heart of champagne country, was one of Europe's truly great road racing circuits. The public roads on which so many great battles took place in the 1950s and 1960s still exist, of course, and some of the race-related buildings, although in disrepair, are regular tourist attractions, but the sound of hairy sports cars at this exciting venue have long since been silenced.

The 906's role as a pure sports racer is endorsed by its use of top-hinged doors. In 1954, when Daimler-Benz launched the mighty 300SL 'Gullwing' with top-hinged doors, a question mark hung over the car's safety. A number of commentators pointed out that escape from the cabin in the unfortunate event of a car being rolled on to its roof would be impossible. The creation of a wind-cheating body took priority over driver safety in the mid-1960s, but, happily, no one had cause to complain about the 906 from this point of view.

Always a favourite spot among professional motor-racing photographers, the Nürburgring's Karussel provides the backdrop for this fine Günther Molter study of Udo Schütz in the short-tailed 906. By the mid-1960s the 906 not only marked a departure from Porsche's normal practice of building dual-purpose cars that doubled as road and race cars, but also saw the return of Germany's national racing colour for this and subsequent works racing Porsches. Metallic silver had been favoured for the pre-war Auto-Union and Mercedes-Benz Grand Prix cars during Hitler's reign in the 1930s, and for many years after the Second World War by both Porsche and Daimler-Benz, but white had always been the German purist's choice.

Chapter 3

TAKE SIX, ANOTHER FOR THE ROAD – PORSCHE 911, 1963–2000

Of all the cars exhibited at the 1963 Frankfurt Auto Show only two, the VW Beetle and Porsche 911, would enjoy an unbroken production run into the twenty-first century. Designed principally by Butzi Porsche, this early 2-litre, six-cylinder 130bhp coupe, originally known as the 901, was the actual launch car, but series production failed to get under way until 1964. A classic by any standards, the new Porsche initially received a mixed reaction from enthusiasts, many of whom did not take to the styling. Others proclaimed that a powerful successor to the long-in-the-tooth four-cylinder 356 was long overdue and, as Porsche's profits have shown all too clearly during the past decades, they were absolutely right.

Introduction

Work began on a successor to the 356 in the early 1960s when Porsche were enjoying hitherto unknown levels of prosperity. Dubbed 901 in Porsche's entirely logical numbering system, the design of the new car was largely the work of Butzi Porsche, who worked under the guidance and influence of styling supremo Erwin Komenda.

As much as sports-car enthusiasts loved the 356, a minority considered that a larger, faster Porsche would be a more fulfilling proposition to meet their motoring needs in the new decade. And Ferry Porsche wholeheartedly concurred.

The 901 made its public debut at the 1963 Frankfurt Auto Show, an exercise aimed at gauging public reaction to the car. This was predictably mixed, and had Porsche become down-hearted by the 901's most loquacious critics, it would not have gone into production in 1964. Many were apt to compare the 901 with the rounded curves of the pretty 356, and declared the new car to be unworthy of its bonnet badge, which was not an especially flattering view. Other, less reactionary, folk, however, took a more considered and rational approach, and recognised Butzi's body styling as a subtle, neatly penned masterpiece. The mechanical specification was equally interesting, and held much promise. Intended as a fast roadgoing sports/GT coupe, with sufficient room behind the front seats to carry a brace of little 'uns, the 901 carried the 356's principal design tenets several steps further.

The all new 2-litre, six-cylinder, horizontally opposed engine sat in the tail with the alloy cased gearbox amidships. Naturally, the power unit was air-cooled, but in place of pushrod actuation of the valves there was a single overhead camshaft for each bank of cylinders. Dry-sump lubrication was also adopted, to prevent the age-old problem of oil 'surge' to one side of the engine under hard cornering.

With a 9:1 compression ratio, maximum power of 130bhp was produced at 6,100rpm, and top speed was in the region of 130mph. Suspension was by torsion bars and struts at the front, and torsion bars and parallel trailing arms at the rear. At the back the 356's pure swing-axle system was dispensed with in favour of narrow driveshafts with universal joints on their ends. This negated the much-exaggerated tendency of the rear wheels to adopt 'tuck-under' during severe cornering at high speeds.

Braking was taken care of by discs, to the same specification as the 356C's, at all four corners, and the 15-in diameter wheels were in steel and closed with chromed hubcaps. At 4.5 in wide the wheels were absurdly narrow, but the standard 165 × 15 radial tyres were a huge improvement over the crossplies of earlier days.

Porsche 356 owner and fanatic Denis Jenkinson, was one of the many people who did not initially take to the 901. Of an early prototype he commented: 'Compared to the 356 series cars, it seemed huge, and while the flat-6 engine was quite pleasant, it was pretty noisy without the excitement of the 2-litre Carrera engine. It was certainly a better engine than the pushrod 4-cylinder, which it should have been, being 400cc larger, but my feeling was that Porsche had taken two steps forward and three backwards.' 'Jenks' considered that it rode quite smoothly, but there was far too much body roll, even under gentle cornering. However, he hit the nail on the head in remarking: 'Instead of looking at it as the beginning of a new era, there was a tendency to view it as another step in the development of the 356, which was totally wrong. What one should have done was to compare it with the 356 of 1950 and then add 10 years of development.'

Like so many others Denis Jenkinson would come in time to regard the 911 as one of the truly great cars of the sporting world. Series production began in 1964, but there were teething problems that needed to be ironed out. The Solex carburettors, which lacked development, suffered from 'flat spots', and not everyone was impressed with the car's handling. Journalists and owners alike complained of excessive oversteer, which was blamed on the rear weight bias. Porsche attempted to solve this problem initially by placing lead weights in the front bumper, whereas the real problem largely lay with the narrow wheels and tyres. Development of the car began almost immediately, as is Porsche's custom, and within a short period the 911, as it was dubbed after Peugeot complained about the 901 appellation, became a most acceptable machine.

Within just four months of the beginning of production, a 911 placed fifth in the Monte-Carlo Rally, an event that it would go on to win outright on four occasions (1968, 1969, 1970 and 1979). Joining the 911 from 1965 was the similarly bodied 912, fitted with the 356's 1.6-litre 90bhp engine. Being considerably cheaper to buy than the six-cylinder car, but boasting a top speed of 115mph, the 912 naturally sold extremely well. Regrettably, it was discontinued in 1969 after the production of 30,300 units.

The German economy made one of its rare dips into recession in the mid-1960s, but curiously this had little impact on Porsche's fortunes. When the range was increased in 1967/68 to include three states of engine tune – 911S (160bhp), 911L (130bhp) and 911T (110bhp) – production began to rise sharply. In 1967 Porsche also began to take the 911 seriously as a circuit racer, and produced the 911R. This was mostly for the benefit of a small number of wealthy privateers, in whose hands the cars enjoyed success at all levels of sports-car racing. Fitted with the 210bhp Carrera 6 engine, the quickest 911Rs paved the way for extraordinary development of the road cars. Those, like Denis Jenkinson, who had been sceptical about the original 901 were rapidly changing their opinion by the late 1960s. 'Jenks' commented:

One thing was clear and that was that no-one was copying Porsche design trends: you could say that Porsche Engineering was forging a lonely path. While the conception of the 911 was everyone's idea of the ideal GT car, most people agreed that if you had to follow the Porsche route, you would be hard pressed to match their design and quality. Porsche Engineering was becoming a by-word for excellence in the automobile world, accepted everywhere as being as near to perfection as was possible, with no short cuts to save money or time.

While the racing department concentrated its efforts on the powerful six-, eight- and twelve-cylinder prototypes during the latter half of the 1960s, the 911 was far from neglected. Indeed, many of the components developed and fitted to prototype racing cars like the 917 would eventually find their way into the road cars.

Along with the regular coupe 911s, there was also the unique Targa, an open-top variant with a prominent roll-hoop finished in stainless steel. This model was never as popular among purists as the coupe, but sufficiently well loved in the sunnier climes of the world to make for extremely healthy production figures.

For 1969 Porsche also launched the Sporto-matic version of the 911, the 'contraption with a gear lever and no clutch pedal', as so many reactionaries dubbed it. This innovative, semi-automatic car was considered by many to be heretical; Porsches were deemed to be proper sports cars, and 'proper' sports car did not have automatic gearboxes. With the wisdom of hindsight the semi-auto version was a great idea, but one that was too far ahead of its time. When the sophisticated Tiptronic semi-automatic gearboxes – developed from the PDK-equipped Group C racing cars of the mid-1980s – appeared on Porsches in the 1990s, driving enthusiasts queued up for them.

In 1970 the 911's engine was enlarged to 2.2 litres, which increased power and torque across the board. The 'S' version produced 180bhp at 6,500rpm and was capable of 138mph. Acceleration was equally impressive, especially mid-range punch – the minimum 0–60mph time took just 7 seconds. Power output was increased again in 1972 when the engine was expanded in capacity to 2.4 litres. This gave customers the option of the 130bhp 911T, 165bhp 911E and 190bhp 911S, with top speeds of 127mph, 138mph and 144mph respectively.

At the same time Porsche also re-introduced the famous Carrera name on a car that would be accorded instant classic status, and be assured of a worldwide 'cult' following. The 2.7-litre lightweight Carrera was created at the suggestion of Dr Ernst Fuhrmann, designer of the original four-cam engine debuted at the Nürburgring in 1953. Developing 210bhp at 6,300rpm the car had a genuine top speed of 152mph, and could easily accelerate from 0–60mph in 5 seconds. With its narrow-gauge steel bodywork, controversial 'ducktail' spoiler, hugely powerful brakes from the 917 and stripped-out, racing-style cabin, the Carrera was, in effect, a fully road-legal racing car.

However, this car was also hugely expensive to buy, which gave Porsche's marketing department deep reservations about the wisdom of the project. Despite this, within a week or two of the car's official launch in Paris, the first batch of 500 cars had been sold, and production of a further 500 was under way. The impression this Carrera made upon the sports-car world is not to be underestimated. A good many journalists were apt to complain about the supposed vagaries of the Porsche's tail-happy handling, but more knowledgeable folk considered the Carrera to be the best car of its day.

While there was public euphoria about the lightweight 2.7-litre car, and its huge success in European and American circuit racing, there were grumblings behind the scenes at Zuffenhausen. Some at Porsche considered the 911 to be in need of a more conventional replacement, and work started on a new breed of front-engined Porsches. Also in 1972 there was the much publicised family 'bust-up'. It had become apparent to Ferry Porsche that there was a power struggle in the company between his children and his sister's children, the Piëchs. Given the nature of families – all families – this squabbling was inevitable. With the frightening and intelligent logic that Ferry applied to everything in his life, he took a large metaphorical stick to the lot of them. Dispossessed of all power, the rows stopped, instantly, and that was that.

Having recovered from this disturbance, Porsche, along with the rest of the motor industry, faced the 1973 Middle East oil crisis, which claimed a number of casualties. Porsche

rode out the storm well because it had wares that people wanted to buy. In the same year the Carrera RSRs performed particularly well in competition, and assured the company of a high profile in the international press. Fitted with special 330bhp 2.8-litre engines these cars dominated the European GT Championship, and scored outright victories in the Daytona 24 Hours and Targa Florio – the last time that the great Sicilian road race was held.

Inspired by BMW's original example, Porsche began experimenting with turbo-charging in the early 1970s. After complete success with the 1,100bhp 917 Spyder in the Can-Am series, the company turbocharged racing versions of the 911. In 1974 a 2.1-litre car developing about 500bhp finished second overall at Le Mans, an incredible result for a GT car initially designed for road use.

Driving these early cars was, for the most part, a fairly odd experience as the turbo suffered from 'lag' and acted like an 'on-off' switch. Power delivery was savage but this problem was overcome, and in 1975 Porsche launched the roadgoing 911 turbo (officially the 930). At this time the regular 911 range was fitted with 2.7-litre engines, but the turbo had a 3-litre unit developing 260bhp at 5,500rpm. With a top speed of 155mph, the car was fast, its torque and acceleration taking motor-car development into a wholly different sphere.

The mid-1970s saw the launch of the 928, a V8 4.5 litre (later enlarged to 5 litres), with conventional water-cooling, four seats and an attractive wind-cheating bodyshell. In official literature this model was desribed as Porsche's new 'flagship', which not only raised a few eyebrows and tempers in the 911 camp, but also made Ferry Porsche occasionally wonder where he had gone wrong. The great man never made any secret of his distaste of this model, nor of the direction in which others were attempting to take his company.

The four-cylinder, 2.5-litre 924 also arrived in the mid-1970s, and was marketed as a high-quality, 'entry-level' sports car designed to broaden Porsche's appeal to younger folk. On the world's race tracks Porsche were winning with cars powered by air-cooled, flat-six engines. Owners of 911s identified closely with the track cars – one reason why the 911 was so successful – but there were some within the company who were heading in a wholly different direction. History would record that it was the wrong one, as Ferry Porsche had known all along.

As a result of the company's foray into the world of automotive convention, development of the 911 was neglected. In 1978 the 911 range comprised the 180bhp, 3-litre SC and the 300bhp, 3.3-litre Turbo. Ironically, it was Porsche's American chief executive Peter Schutz who was ultimately responsible for halting the decline of the 911. Porsche's most important export markets had always been in the USA where, since the days of the 356, the company had gained a loyal following.

To Peter Schutz the future of Porsche was inconceivable without the rear-engined car. On one occasion he walked into an office occupied by Porsche's chief technical director, Professor Helmut Bott, and saw a bar chart on the wall. This clearly showed that Bott, and others, intended production of the 924 and 928 to go on and on, while the end of the 911 had been marked for 1981. Schutz, evidently unimpressed, picked up a piece of chalk and, with an angry flourish on the bar chart, indicated that 911 production would be extended well beyond 1981! He then immediately ordered a new model – the 911 Cabriolet – to be built. This, the first true cabriolet since the 356, was first shown as a design study at the 1981 Frankfurt Auto Show; reaction to it was so favourable that the car was rushed into production for the 1983 model year. Needless to say, it became an instant success.

In 1981 Porsche also fielded a team of 924s for Le Mans. Schutz, a shrewd businessman who knew little of the technical side of cars, asked if these cars stood a chance of outright victory at the Sarthe. Inevitably, Schutz was correctly informed that the 924s stood no chance whatever of winning, as they were pitted against thoroughbred racing cars. Once again the American saw red. Of this he commented: 'As long as I am going to be president of this organisation, we'll never go to any race without

the object of winning.' Schutz's influence was considerable, for after this verbal delivery the company built the all-conquering 956 Group C cars, and spent most of the 1980s comprehensively demonstrating what 'all-conquering' really meant. By the end of the 1980s Ferry Porsche breathed something of a sigh of relief and publicly commented: 'I say quite openly that we would be in a very bad position today if the 911 had been discontinued. I am absolutely clear in my mind about that.'

As 911 sales picked up, the traditional production car came to the fore once again. In 1984 the Carrera version of the 911 was treated to the 3.2-litre, 231bhp engine, and was also made available with the turbo's widearched body and 'whale-tale' rear spoiler.

Utilising new technology, largely developed by Porsche, an advanced four-wheel-drive version of the 911 – the Group B 959 – appeared as a design study at the Frankfurt Auto Show in 1983. With a 2.8-litre, twin-turbo flat-six developing 450bhp, a team of these cars was prepared for the tough Paris–Dakar Raid in 1986, and duly recorded the first outright victory for a sports car in this event. A racing 961 version was also entered for Le Mans in 1986, and timed at 198mph down through Mulsanne. In 1987/88, 283 examples of the 959 were built in road trim and released to selected customers, who considered themselves to be very lucky indeed.

In 1988 the company also revived the famous Speedster name for a wickedly attractive version of the 911. With its 'cutdown' windscreen and rear tonneau cover, its styling closely aped the original version of the 356 Speedster of the mid-1950s. For the following year the 911 was completely revised as the 964, and fitted with a beautiful 250bhp, 3.6-litre version of the classic, air-cooled flatsix. Some 87 per cent of the car was completely new, although it was unmistakably a 911, and came with ABS brakes, and the option of the four-wheel-drive Carrera 4 variant.

Although the 964's aesthetics were controversial – the bumpers particularly gave the car something of a flabby appearance – the international press revived its interest in Porsches. As a result of the electronics revolution in the motor industry, the 911 was becoming sophisticated and even more finely honed. This, however, did not satisfy a few journalists who grumbled about the 911's rear weight bias, and tricky wet-weather handling. In reality it was anything but difficult; complex changes to the suspension geometry had long since led to the creation of a rear-engined car with completely neutral cornering manners.

By the end of the 1980s Porsche's Group C sports racing programme had come to an end. Jaguar, Mercedes-Benz and Peugeot had spent vast sums on increasingly sophisticated cars that were aimed at toppling the Porsche 962. Porsche had proved its point by winning every major competition time and again and, as the financial stakes were raised and the rules governing sports-car racing rewritten, Porsche's effort at the top level faded away.

This had a dramatic effect on the development and popularity of the 911. In 1986 Porsche inaugurated the Porsche Cup, a highly popular racing series for 911 owners. The competition was tough and the racing close, which pleased spectators. As the Cup series grew in stature Porsche built increasingly powerful and dramatic-looking cars for circuit work, and once more the 911 was in ascendance. In 1990 the racing series became known as the Carrera Cup, and there was a new car, the Carrera 2. In Cup form this was 170kg lighter than the standard road version but, like the latter, the race car was notable for its three-way catalytic converter and use of unleaded fuel.

For 1992 Porsche launched the lightweight Carrera RS, a pure road car that was clearly inspired by the Cup versions. Some 150kg lighter than the regular 911, the Carrera RS's 3.6-litre engine was rated at 260bhp; it was, of course, seriously fast with a top speed of 162mph and the ability to sprint to 60mph in 5 seconds. A year later, though, this was slightly overshadowed by the advent of the 3.6-litre Turbo, which, with 360bhp, boasted almost racing-car performance.

The Turbo's acceleration from 90mph to its limit of 170mph was fairly incomprehensible to normal mortals, and like the original Turbo of 1975, had to be experienced to be believed. A special Turbo S version, with 18 in diameter wheels and 381bhp, was also available for the benefit of a small minority who sought the kind of voltage that can only otherwise be gained from taunting Nile crocodiles at close quarters.

For the 1994 model year the 911 was completely revised again, with new, 'active' rear suspension, a 272bhp version of the flat-six and sensational body styling. Codenamed 993, many regarded this version of the 911 as the best looking of the entire breed. There were two- and four-wheel-drive versions, and from 1995 there was a spiritual successor to the 1972 2.7-litre Carrera lightweight in the form of the Carrera RS. For their lucky owners the Carrera RS took the concept of fun motoring into a wholly new dimension.

Naturally, there were no concessions to luxury, and the car only weighed 1,270kg, but these factors, in conjunction with 300bhp, resulted in what many have come to regard as the most desirable Porsche road car ever. Without turbocharging power, response from the engine was instant and massive. At roughly the same time Porsche also launched the twin-turbocharged Turbo model, with four-wheel drive and 408bhp, a new version of the Targa with an ingenious sliding glass roof, and the utterly stunning GT2. The latter was intended as a competition model, but road-legal versions were no less impressive. Fitted with a massive 'bi-plane' rear wing, these cars arguably represent the ultimate expression on the pure 911 theme, and were largely responsible for maintaining worldwide interest in this venerable classic.

With sales of the 911 increasing once more by the 1990s, Porsche finally pulled the plug on the front-engined 928. This formidable and competent Grand Touring car was the equal of contemporary sports tourers from Daimler-Benz, but was never wholly accepted by the Porsche fraternity. The original proponents of the 928 at the Zuffenhausen factory, who considered that it would provide for Porsche's future, had been wrong. Ferry Porsche was too much of a gentleman, though, to have made pithy remarks about the whimsical ideas of youngsters who thought that they knew better than he did.

In 1996 the company pulled off yet another masterstroke with the launch of the pretty mid-engined, two-seater Boxster. The styling of this machine harked back to the 718 RSK of the late 1950s, and the purchase price squared it with two-seaters from Lotus, Daimler-Benz and BMW. Fitted with a 2.5-litre, 204bhp, water-cooled flat-six, top speed was an impressive 149mph, or 146mph for the automatic Tiptronic version.

Above all else, the Boxster broadened Porsche's appeal to reach a much wider audience, particularly younger folk. The car is considerably cheaper to buy then a 911, but is as quick as the 1972 lightweight Carrera. Available as a soft-top, or with a hard-top at extra cost, the Boxster considerably increased Porsche's fortunes in the late 1990s, and its popularity shows no signs of abating.

In 1996 Porsche rejoined international sports-car racing at top level with the GT1. This special bore more than a passing resemblance to the 911, but had a 600bhp version of the flat-six and was intended as a serious challenger to McLaren's domination of the world series. For Le Mans 1996 a GT1 narrowly missed overall victory, finishing just one lap behind the winning prototype Porsche WSC 95. At the 1997 Sarthe event a brace of GT1s were placed first and second for most of the race, but gremlins struck and victory once again went to a prototype Porsche. Dramatic in every sense, Porsche built road versions of the GT1, but their eyewatering purchase price has ensured that ownership is fairly exclusive.

In 1997 the beautiful 993 version of the 911 was, regrettably, shelved. Its place was taken by a new-generation 911 (the 996), which almost wholly altered the concept of the car. The engine was still in the rear, although water-cooled, and the body styling was, of course, unmistakable, but, bristling with electronic gadgetry, many considered that it had lost character. Porsche's claim that it was designed to be driven at over 180mph in complete safety is perfectly valid. For example, the car's braking capability, at any speed, in any given situation, on any road surface, is shattering and completely without histrionics. And there is equally impressive acceleration and road-holding to match. The car is a technical *tour de force* – possibly the finest ever expression of automotive engineering – and sales figures have demonstrated that Porsche were right to build it.

In 1999 the company celebrated a record financial year, but, unfortunately, without Ferry Porsche. The great man passed away in 1998 at the age of eighty-eight, having accomplished so much. Considering that his cars had contributed such a great deal to motoring life, both on and off the track, in the twentieth century, his obituaries in the British specialist journals were surprisingly brief.

Porsche was an honest man, and a forward-thinking engineer who, like his father before him, had little time for the irritating mediocrity of meaningless waffle. Some of the company's creations under Ferry Porsche might not have been among the most beautiful automotive machines but, like the man at the helm, at least they always worked properly.

Today, the 8,000 people who work at the factory are busier than ever, because they make cars that people continue to want to buy. They are extraordinarily good cars, as Porsches always have been, but the company not only performs its prime function of building the best sports cars. It is, to be brutally candid, a model of industrial efficiency, and in stark contrast to the many branches of the British motor industry.

From time to time Ferry Porsche's wife Dodo used to remind the old boy of an idea that she held dear to her heart, namely, that 'the future is never as good as we hope, nor as bad as we fear'. There are no worries about the future of Porsche but, with world legislatures threatening our use of motor cars, change is afoot, but it will not be as awful as some imagine.

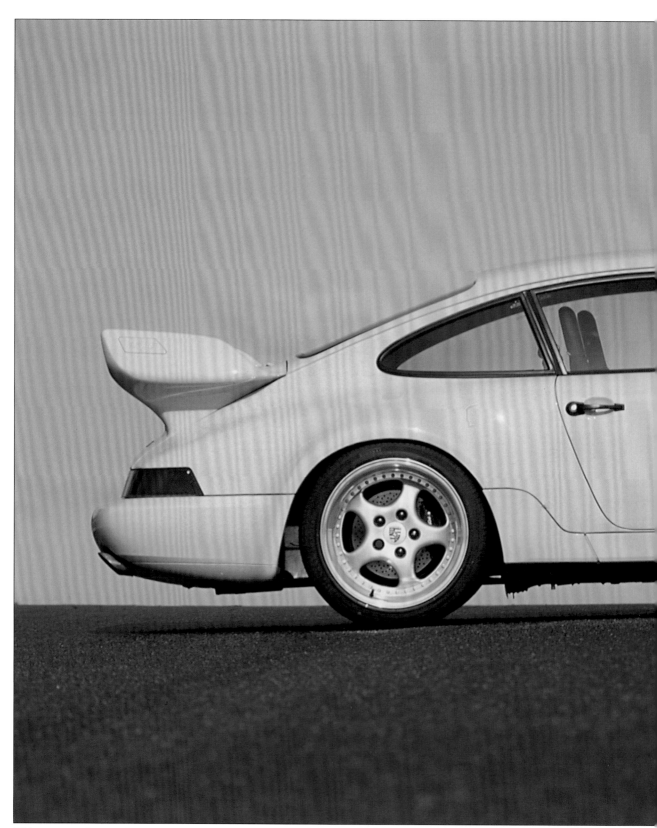

Thirty years after the first of the six-cylinder 901s appeared at Frankfurt, Porsche produced this stunning 3.8-litre 911 Carrera RS. Developing 300bhp at 6,500rpm, this amazing creation was capable of nigh-on 170mph and accelerating from 0–60mph in 4.9 seconds, a big improvement over the original car's top speed of 131mph and ability to sprint to 60mph from rest in

8.5 seconds. Despite huge improvements in power output, braking, aerodynamic stability and roadholding, the classic 911 shape has been faithfully adhered to throughout.

Wind-tunnel testing of a prototype demonstrated that the 901 had a lower drag co-efficient than the outgoing 356, despite the replacement model's greater frontal area. With careful attention to detail the cd figure came down from 0.398 to 0.380. With tufts of wool attached to this prototype – note the twin bank of air-intake louvres on the rear lid – it is clearly shown that even quite small protruding items, like the door handles, can have quite a dramatic effect on the direction of airflow over the car. The science of aerodynamics has, of course, progressed considerably since 1963, but theory is still open to question, particularly in top-level racing-car design.

With their vented 4.5J × 15 steel wheels and chromed hubcaps, the early production 911s looked elegant, or plain, depending on your point of view. A more sophisticated and complex car than the 356 in almost every respect, the coupe was intended as a rapid sports-cum-GT, and one that showed great competition potential almost from the earliest days. In true sporting fashion the 'cammy' engine demanded constant use of the gear stick to get the best out of the car, a facet of the 911 that drivers revelled in and some American journalists criticised.

This beautifully prepared 911 was entered for the 1965 Monte-Carlo Rally. Fitted with no fewer than five additional driving lamps, and heavily treaded snow tyres, the car was driven by Herbert Linge and Peter Falk who finished fifth overall. The 911's 44/56 front-to-rear weight distribution gave a distinct advantage in rallying, as the bias in the tail endowed the 911 with the ability to change direction extremely quickly in corners. Linge and Falk's fifth place was a creditable rookie debut in international rallying, but there were greater things to come. Porsche 911s would go on to win the Monte on no fewer than four occasions. Note the Porsche 356 and rear-engined NSU Prinz.

The distinctive Targa version was added to the range in 1966. This variant was not a 'rag-top' in the strictest sense, but a safety inspired compromise with a removable roof panel and sturdy roll-bar with a stainless-steel finish. Butzi Porsche had originally wanted the steel hoop to have a matt-black finish, but his idea was not taken up until the mid-1970s. Note that the early examples had a zipped rear window in plastic; later cars had a fixed, glass item.

The 1.6-litre, four-cylinder 912 debuted in 1965 as an inexpensive alternative to the six-cylinder 911. Developing 90bhp, the 912's engine was the same unit that had been fitted to the 356 Super 90 and gave the new car a top speed in the region of 115mph. As the four-cylinder engine was appreciably lighter than the flat-six, the 912's handling was virtually foolproof. It was a nice car that remains undervalued today. This 1967 example is fitted with Fuchs alloy wheels, which were standard on the 911S from 1967 and available as an extra-cost option on other models.

Introduced in 1967, the 911S provided the first evidence that the six-cylinder Porsche had a great deal of development potential. The 2-litre engine had a rise in compression ratio – from 9:1 to 9.8:1, the valve diameters were increased and there were larger Weber 40IDS3C carburettors. These fundamental changes boosted engine power from 130bhp at 6,100rpm to 160bhp at 6,600rpm, endowing the 'S' with a potential top speed of 137mph, and a minimum 0–60mph time of about 8 seconds. For a steel-bodied car with a 2-litre engine these were astonishing figures by 1967 standards; journalists and 'Porschephiles' alike suddenly aspired to 911S ownership.

An official Porsche publicity shot identifying 911S ownership with a new business élite who were successful in the fledgling global economy. Air travel in 1968 was, of course, extremely rare for all except the well heeled, and illustrations like this were intended to create the impression – real or imaginary – that 'high-fliers' led a lifestyle to which all 'right-minded' folk under the age of thirty-five aspired. How things would change in the 1970s!

In 1968 Porsche added two more 911s to the line-up in the form of the 110bhp 911T and the 130bhp 911L. Both were fitted with the same basic 2-litre engines, but in different states of tune. The fuel-injected 911E, developing 140bhp, would debut in the following year. A minority of journalists considered the 'entry-level' 911T to be under-powered, despite its top speed of 124mph and ability to sprint to 60mph in 8.3 seconds, but slowly began to recognise the merits of Porsche engineering when in the 1970s British Leyland launched the mighty 3.5-litre V8 version of the MGB. The MG was fast and powerful, but gave similar performance figures to the 911T. To reiterate, the British car had a 3.5-litre V8 engine!

The 2-litre 911L, seen here in a sombre shade of 'washing-up-bowl' beige, was intended as the luxury, mid-range car between the 911T (T for Touring) and the sporting 'S' version. Like the early 911, it developed 130bhp at 6,100rpm, and a useful 176Nm of torque at 4,200rpm. With a top speed in excess of 130mph and punchy acceleration, particularly between 65–90mph, it was a most rewarding and civilised car, capable of high average cross-country speeds. These cars were also way ahead of their time in terms of primary and secondary safety, concepts that the anti-car lobby has wholeheartedly failed to grasp.

Porsche's sports-racing effort during 1968 centred around development of the eight-cylinder 907/908 prototypes, which were astonishingly successful all season. Pictured here is the great English driver Vic Elford during his epic drive in the Targa Florio in the regular short-tailed 907. At one stage Elford lost a full 17 minutes fitting the spare wheel, but made up time at an astonishing pace – breaking the lap record in the process – to record Porsche's eighth outright victory in the Sicilian classic. Elford's drive, one of the greatest in motor-racing history, was recorded in great detail in the international press, and undoubtedly aided sales of the 911 road cars.

In 1968 Porsche also prepared a number of 911s for the London–to–Sydney Marathon, the first, and arguably the most difficult, of the modern long-distance rallies. The Polish driver, Sobieslav Zasada, who had previously enjoyed a number of victories with Porsches in rallying, took this example, seen here at an historic meeting at the Nürburgring in 1981, to a spirited fourth overall. The Sydney was won by a Hillman Hunter which, all things considered, was a quite remarkable feat. During 1968 Vic Elford took 911s to victory in both the Monte-Carlo and British RAC Rallies, and Rolls-Royce's chief engineer Harry Grylls, who had been responsible for the Silver Shadow, bought a VW Beetle in which to enjoy motoring in retirement . . .

By 1969 911 developments had included the introduction of laminated windscreens, larger door handles, dual brake cylinders, wider wheels and a host of other improvements. The unloved Sportomatic version, with a semi-automatic gearbox, was launched and the 912, seen here with steel wheels and hubcaps, was temporarily discontinued. American exhaust-emissions legislation began to have an important effect on engine and fuel-management design, but Porsche would strive successfully to keep ahead of developments in the White House.

In 1969 Porsche gave notice that the company would no longer be playing second fiddle to Ford, or anyone else, in sports-car racing, and promptly launched the fearsome and totally outrageous 917. A milestone car in every sense, the original 4.5-litre, horizontally opposed, air-cooled, twelve-cylinder engine developed about 600bhp. Capable of nearly 250mph, the 917 was not especially successful in its maiden year; drivers were understandably frightened of it because, until John Wyer took a

hacksaw to the tail and fitted a more appropriate, upturned spoiler, the car's handling was nervous and unpredictable above 200mph. With the bugs ironed out Porsche won its first outright victory at Le Mans in 1970, and again in 1971, victories that once more sharply increased sales of both Porsche's road cars and Volkswagen's immortal Beetle. Incidentally, the 1970 Le Mans-winning 917 was offered for sale in February 2000 for a cool £2.2 million.

The glamour of the Targa, with a fixed, glass rear window by 1968/69, is captured in this dazzling publicity shot. Despite similar performance potential to the regular 'tin-top' coupes, Targas never found favour with Porsche purists. They did not wholly take to the styling and argued in any case that the coupe was far more wholesome than the fresh-air variant. Interestingly, Targas exchange hands nowadays for roughly 10 per cent less than their coupe counterparts.

The 917 was as far removed from ordinary road cars, and even powerful ones like the 911, as could be imagined at the end of the 1960s. Nothing like it had been seen since the awe-inspiring Auto-Union and Mercedes-Benz Grand Prix cars that trounced everything in the 1930s. Capable of accelerating to 60mph in bottom gear in well under 3 seconds, most examples were fitted with just one part that was interchangeable with the humble VW Beetle – the latter's cardboard ducting, attached to the engine fan housing and heat exchangers, was employed to guide cooling air into the 917's cockpit to enhance driver comfort in hot weather. Count Rossi of the Martini drinks concern had a car similar to the JW Automotive 917, seen here, registered for road use!

Known affectionately as 'screamers', the last of the classic 2-litre 911s were built in 1970 at a time when the Zuffenhausen company's fortunes were riding high and rising. Influential journalists, like *Motor Sport*'s Denis Jenkinson, after initially criticising the early cars, considered the 911S to be among the very best sports cars, but rejected owning one on the grounds of the car's complexity. In any case, Jenks admitted publicly on several occasions that he had been completely corrupted by the formidable torque of his 4.2-litre Jaguar E-Type.

Debuted in 1969, the mid-engined VW-Porsche 914 two-seater replaced the unsuccessful Karmann Ghia Type 34 'razor-edge', and was built on the same production line at Karmann's plant in Osnabrück. Originally fitted with Volkswagen's 1,679cc twin-carburettor engine – the example seen here is a later 2-litre car – few inside the Porsche fold warmed to its quirky styling, and even fewer to its Volkswagen performance. The 914/4's top speed of 109mph and 0–60mph capability of 13.9 seconds were not comparable with contemporary sports cars, and sales were initially slow.

In 1969 Porsche also launched the six-cylinder 914/6, which proved to be an altogether more satisfactory, if extremely expensive, car. Fitted with the 911's 2-litre, 110bhp, flat-six, top speed was increased to 125mph, and the best 0–60mph time tumbled to 8 seconds. The 914/6's principal advantage over the 911 was its mid-engined configuration, which inevitably gave the car higher levels of grip in corners. Despite Porsche's heavy commitment to the 917 project, the 914/6 was homologated for racing in 1970 and several cars were prepared for battle.

The 914/6 GT, which was made available to private entrants, was distinguishable from the standard 914/4 by its Fuchs 6-in-wide alloy wheels and wide wheel arches. In addition there were fibreglass front and rear lids, stiffer suspension with reduced ride height and an extremely powerful 210bhp version of the 911's engine behind the driver's backside. Painted in white and black, one example, driven by Guy Chasseuil and Claude Ballot-Lena, was entered by the French Sonauto team for Le Mans in 1970. Much of the race was held in wet weather, and the little car kept going, while so many others fell by the wayside. At the finish the Porsche crossed the line in a quite remarkable sixth overall, scoring a class win into the bargain.

A team of 914/6 GTs was entered for the 1970 endurance event the Marathon de la Route, in which Porsche had enjoyed past success. Engines were tuned to 160bhp to ensure reliability. The three cars, their bumpers painted in different colours for easy recognition by pit crews, finished in first, second and third places – a convincing demonstration. Between them the winning drivers, Gerard Larousse, Claude Haldi and Dr Helmut Marko, covered 6,293 miles in 86 hours over the punishing Nürburgring track. Long-since defunct events like this lend weight to the oft-vented argument that modern Formula 1 races, which last for approximately 90 minutes, are something of a waste of effort.

For 1971 Porsche opted to run a team of 914/6 GTs in the 1971 Monte-Carlo Rally, held in some of the worst weather in the Monte's history. With superior traction the 911 would have been a better bet, but the mid-engined cars had to be tried – a big mistake as it turned out. Rear-engined Renault Alpine A110s filled the first three places, Porsche's conclusion being that the 914 was eminently more suited to road racing than rallying. The cars seen here are being prepared prior to the Monte.

A number of special versions of the 914/6 were made during the early 1970s including this attractive creation. The car was commissioned by Verne Ben Heidrich, styled by Pietro Frua of Italy and built by Hispano-Aleman. 'Pop-up' headlamps and the Porsche badge were retained on the nosecone, but there are few other give-aways that this is a Porsche under the skin.

The Frua-styled 914/6 was very much in keeping with contemporary Italian fashion, the 'flying buttresses' above the rear wings being similar in concept to those of the mid-engined Ferrari Dino 246 and Maserati Merak. The window-glass area is commendably large, the alloy wheels ornate in typically Italian style and there's a neat engine air-intake in each of the rear wings behind the doors.

In 1972 Porsche built the 916, a superb car with aggressively wide wheel arches, 7J × 15 Fuchs alloy wheels, fixed steel roof panel (there was no Targa version) and a front spoiler and side skirts. Engines included the 190bhp 2.4-litre 911 unit, and the 210bhp, 'lump' that saw service in the lightweight Carreras, also built in 1972. These cars were seriously fast and had impressive looks, but the project was shelved after the construction of just eleven examples. With a projected purchase price in North America of $14,000, it was simply far too expensive a proposition.

The most special of the 914 breed, officially the 914S but more popularly dubbed as the 914/8, was this stunning mechanical creation of 1969. Two such cars were built, this example for Ferry Porsche – his sixtieth birthday present – and an orange one for Dr Ferdinand Piëch. An opening below the front bumper for the oil cooler distinguishes the car externally, but under the rear lid of this silver car is a detuned version of the 3-litre, flat-eight engine from the 908 sports racing car.

Ferry Porsche's eight-cylinder car was fitted with four 46-mm Weber carburettors instead of fuel injection, and developed in the region of a relatively paltry 260bhp at 7,700rpm. Dr Piëch's example, on the other hand, had Bosch fuel injection and 300bhp at a maximum of 7,500rpm – some 50bhp less than the full-blown racing unit due to the

power-sapping nature of the road-legal exhaust system. Although the glorious eight-cylinder engines were not especially prone to setting themselves on fire, both Porsche and Piëch's cars had their front luggage compartments filled with fire extinguishers.

Porsche dropped the 914/6 in 1972 and replaced it with the 2-litre, four-cylinder car. Developing 100bhp, this version was good for 118mph, and 0–60mph in 10 seconds, but it was discontinued in 1975. A further model with a 1.8-litre engine debuted in 1974. This was the same fuel-injected unit employed in the Volkswagen Type 411E; developing 80bhp, it endowed the car with a top speed of 109mph. Although the 2-litre model bowed out in 1975, the 1.8-litre continued in production for a further twelve months when it was replaced by the front-engined 2-litre 924.

In 1970 Porsche increased the engine capacity of the 911 from 2 to 2.2 litres, which resulted in an increase in power and torque across the entire range. The three models, 911T, 911E and 911S, developed 125bhp, 155bhp and 180bhp respectively, sufficient to endow even the entry-level model with a top speed of 127mph, and the 'S' with the potential to reach 138mph. By 1970 pop idol Jimi Hendrix was dead from a drugs overdose, politicians promised that nuclear power would solve the world's energy problems, the Vietnam War had fizzled out and the word 'environment' (*umwelt* in German) had crept into the vocabulary of the growing anti-car lobby. American legislation governing exhaust emissions would result in larger capacity engines from several sports-car manufacturers and as much air pollution as ever.

At the end of the 1960s Porsche rejuvenated the age-old idea of a four-seater Porsche and created this prototype. With full marks for total lack of imagination the car was a slightly longer version of the regular 911 with an extended rear side window. Fitted with the 911S's 2.2-litre, 180bhp engine the four-seater naturally had superb performance, but it did not go into production for the best possible reason – there was no need for a four-seater 911. Lamborghini launched their V12 Espada – also a four-seater – at about this time, a car that largely proved Porsche were right to stick to their guns.

Porsche also commissioned Pininfarina to build a four-seater version of the 911, accomplished with rather better results than Porsche's own effort. The rear side window has an upswept trailing edge, with louvres cut into the panel behind it, to give a more integrated and squat shape. This style of rear side window would eventually be used in the Mk2 VW Passat and Lancia Beta saloons, but never on a Porsche.

As was Porsche's usual practice, the 911 race and rally programme kept well ahead of developments with the road cars. This 2.4-litre car was prepared for the 1970 Tour de France, a full two years before the 2.4-litre engine was available to customers at the showroom.

For 1972 the production cars had engines increased in capacity to 2,341cc, but were badged as 2.4 litres for convenience. Design of the new engines was centred around the need to run on low-octane fuel and reduce exhaust emissions, and the compression ratio was lowered across the entire range. Despite this there was a useful gain in both power and torque across the range, the 911S pushing out a purposeful 190bhp at 6,500rpm. Top speed for this car was in the region of 144mph, with 60mph arriving from standstill in a best time of 6.6 seconds. In this same year the 'S' was fitted with a front chin spoiler, an extra-cost option on the other models.

Porsche fielded several cars in the East African Safari Rally during the 1970s, but outright victory proved elusive. Bjorn Waldegaard ought to have won the 1971 event in this 2.2-litre car, but retired after crashing into the similar 911 driven by Zasada, who eventually finished fifth. Waldegaard was a superb driver but not even he could cope with the dust storms of the 1971 event. Naturally, Porsche's inability to achieve outright victory in the Safari led to a great deal of sniggering among the Volkswagen fraternity at this time; Beetles had won this difficult event, without works backing, on no fewer than four occasions!

A baronial setting for this official publicity shot of the 1972 range of Porsches, with a 911S with chin spoiler (left), 914 (centre) and 911 Targa (right). At the beginning of the 1970s Porsche introduced a new range of bright colours, the reds, yellows and oranges being entirely appropriate for sports cars of this era, but retained the more conservative browns and blacks for customers who, quite understandably, never warmed to the idea of Porsche's completely unforgettable shade of Roman Purple.

Test cars pose for the camera prior to a thrash around the Black Forest in the summer sunshine of 1973. For sports-car enthusiasts, especially those employed by the factory, these were exciting times, as the roads of many European countries were relatively free of mobile chicanes and petrol was cheap. The widespread introduction of financial credit at this time, though, which dramatically increased car ownership, and the after effects of the Middle East oil crisis, would result in a changed motoring world by 1974.

Prior to the 1973 oil crisis, which led to fuel rationing in so many European countries, the Porsche 911 retained its graceful, pure shape, while under the skin it represented everything that was great and good about Zuffenhausen engineering thinking. There were no gadgets, no frills and no gimmicks. What you saw is what you got – an unpretentious driver's car in the best Porsche tradition. However, as this decade wore on, not even Porsche could ignore the developments taking place in the motor industry. The 911, too, would eventually put on weight by dint of superfluous items like electrically powered windows and headlamp washers – none of which appealed to traditional clienetele – but the 911 would survive despite the meddlings of marketing folk.

The car that proved the marketing men wrong! In 1972 Porsche revived the Carrera name and launched the 210bhp, 2.7-litre, lightweight 911. Devoid of creature comforts, including a glovebox lid and interior carpeting, it was expensive, raucous and fast, and frightened the living daylights out of the sales department, who were charged with responsibility for selling the first batch of 500. As is well known, this was only the beginning of the 911 Carrera story, for a second batch of 500 was under way within a fortnight of the car's launch. Expensive Carreras have been with us ever since.

Initially available in white, with a choice of blue, red or green side lettering and wheels, the Carreras were distinguished by the 'ducktail' spoiler moulded into the engine lid. This appendage was a necessary aerodynamic aid, which improved the car's high-speed stability and aided traction under hard acceleration. With a top speed of 152mph, and 0–60mph capability of 5.8 seconds, the 2.7-litre lightweight achieved instant classic status, and was so competently engineered that it was instantly race competitive without the need for further modifications. Butzi Porsche did not approve of the 'ducktail', but that was tough luck.

A pair of 2.7-litre Carreras was entered for the 1973 East African Safari Rally. Despite meticulous attention to detail and preparation, both examples retired. In 1974 Bjorn Waldegaard fielded a similar car, and was well in the lead for much of the rally, but driveshaft failure saw him slip into second place at the finish. The humble Beetles in the background might have been a better bet.

Throughout 1973 and 1974 Carreras were particularly successful in GT racing on both sides of the Atlantic. With special racing versions enlarged to 2.8 litres, and by 1974 to a full 3 litres, these 300bhp cars were virtually unbeatable. They were also comparatively easy to drive, dependable and immensely safe. With brakes similar in design to the 917's, stopping power was phenomenal in such a lightweight car; more important from a customer's point of view, the huge success of these cars led directly to much improved road versions.

Sponsored by Martini and painted in the drinks company's attractive and distinctive livery, 2.8- and 3-litre versions of the Carrera RSRs were campaigned in various top-level events throughout 1973. Notable victories included the Daytona 24 Hours and the very last Targa Florio, both of which were surprising wins. Pitted against pukka sports prototypes, the 911 proved that it had the legs, reliability and superior handling of them all. In 1970 Porsche had won the Targa with a purpose-built, short-wheelbase, lightweight Spyder version of the 908; Jo Siffert and Brian Redman were successful with an average speed of 74.66mph. In 1973 the Müller/Van Lennep-winning 911 had averaged 71.11mph in a car with a bodyshell predominately built of steel!

The lightweight Carrera's 2.7-litre engine gave inspiration for another generation of 911s, fitted with similar capacity units, but in different stages of tune. As in the past there were three models, introduced piecemeal from 1974 with 150bhp, 165bhp and the 911S with 175bhp. Increasing weight and exhaust-emissions equipment were, however, beginning to take their toll. The range-topping 'S' was capable of no more than 142mph, which was less than the 2.4-litre version. The car seen here is the 1972 911S 2.7 prototype.

Between the early and mid-1970s Porsche's road-car development was divided between people within the company who wanted to see an end to the 911, and 'loyalists' who wanted to increase its potential. This 2.1-litre Carrera RSR, driven by Van Lennep and Müller at Le Mans 1973, differed from all other 911s in that it was fitted with a turbocharger. This means of forced induction had been 'rediscovered' by BMW in the late 1960s, and began a revolution in increased engine power output. While top entries at Le Mans included the prototype Matras and Ferraris, Porsche fielded two turbocharged 911s in the second-string GT class; while one car ran out of fuel, the Van Lennep/Müller car placed fourth overall. Thereafter, sports-car racing dipped into the doldrums, as politics dictated in favour of the rise of Formula 1.

The beautiful 2.7-litre 1974 Carrera Targa in classic pose with its glorious five-spoke Fuchs alloy wheels and matt-black roll-hoop. By this stage the 911 had been changed to take account of tight parking spaces in urban areas. The front and rear bumpers – the rear fitted with huge rubber-covered overriders – were made more prominent and spring-loaded. Designed to deform and reform during and after 5mph 'shunts', the deformation zones were highlighted with rubber concertinas, a workmanlike solution to appease American safety legislation.

By the mid-1970s the basic 911s remained exciting to drive, but looked a little tired. High-back seats with integral head restraints 'cheapened' the look of the cabin, and 'cookie-cutter' alloy wheels were hardly an improvement over the Fuchs five-spoke alloys, but sales remained healthy enough. Behind the scenes the company was preparing for the launch of a new, front-engined breed of cars, and a production version of the Porsche 911 turbo.

The mid-1970s mid-range 2.7-litre 911 developed 165bhp at 5,800rpm, was well capable of 135mph and 0–60mph in 7.8 seconds. Then, as now, travelling at 135mph is not to be sniffed at, but it is a figure that many contemporary luminaries, particularly from Ferrari and Lamborghini, could easily beat, and blasé journalists not only began to criticise the car for being outdated but, worst of all, many simply ignored it.

One Porsche that no one could fail to notice though, was the 911 Turbo (or 930), publicly debuted in 1974. With its distinctive 'whale-tail' rear spoiler, wide wheel arches, fat wheels and Pirelli tyres, this incarnation of the 911 was truly stunning in every respect. Originally fitted with the 3-litre flat-six (and four-speed gearbox), developing 260bhp at 5,500rpm, it had a top speed of 155mph and 0–60mph capacity of 6 seconds. From 1978 a 3.3-litre engine debuted and top speed rose to 161mph. This figure was academic by this time, but above all the Turbo redefined the concept of all sports machines. It went, stopped and steered better than anything else, and still feels modern by today's standards.

In company with the Turbo and 911 Targa the newcomer to the Porsche fold, the front-engined 924, was launched in the mid-1970s as a successor to the VW-Porsche 914. Designed by Porsche, but built by Audi and fitted with a version of the 2-litre, four-cylinder Volkswagen LT Transporter engine, this 'entry-level' car was designed to appeal to younger folk and those who wanted to own a Porsche but whose pockets would not stretch to one of the rear-engined cars. Much maligned and wholly misunderstood by the ignorant, the 924 utilised many Volkswagen Beetle components, and was criticised for this reason. That Beetle components were made to a standard that most manufacturers could only aspire to continues to escape the attention of many people.

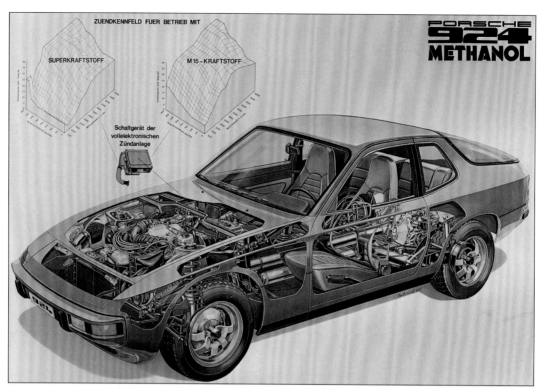

A detailed cut-away illustrating the water-cooled four-cylinder engine up front, long propshaft to the gearbox and transaxle at the rear – an arrangement that gave near 50/50 front-to-rear weight distribution – and relatively simple layout of the suspension. At the front there are the ubiquitous MacPherson struts and coil springs, while semi-trailing arms from the VW Beetle 1303S were used at the rear. Beetle brake discs and drums were fitted front and rear respectively. A 2+2 with a lift-up rear window, the 924 was a practical, economical, well-mannered car with a creditable top speed of 125mph and superb handling.

A perfectly good car with an image problem among aficionados, the 924's biggest problem was that journalists and others, who should have known better, were apt to compare it with more powerful and exotic Porsches. Doyen of motoring scribes, Denis Jenkinson, for example, commented: 'When driving the various versions of the 924, you were always conscious of the fact that the car was not a true Porsche, and you tended to keep saying to yourself, "This is very good for a sports Audi, and some things are pure Porsche, but the overall package is not very impressive."' Seasoned 924 enthusiasts, and there are thousands, are well aware that 'Jenks' was wholly and utterly wrong on this occasion.

Launched in 1978, the 240bhp, 4.5-litre V8 928 was built to compete with the big Mercedes-Benz SL Grand Tourers, and was to the same dimensions. It was the product of new management thinking at Porsche and was intended to be the company's flagship. As a powerful, comfortable 160mph machine, capable of carrying four adults in unruffled luxury and complete safety, it had few rivals, but, in reality, it was not a flagship. This accolade belonged to the 911 Turbo. Ferry Porsche never made any secret of his dislike for this model and, when it was voted Car of the Year, he did not attend the ceremony.

Ferry Porsche was presented with this special 928 prototype – a full four-seater – with its roof extended at the rear, as a seventy-fifth birthday present in September 1984. When Ferdinand Piëch joined Audi, he had plans to make a V10 engine for the 928; this, in effect, would have been the result of joining together two in-line five-cylinder engines from the Audi quattro. This would have undoubtedly been an interesting exercise, particularly as Grand Prix designers were to take the V10 power route in future years, but Ferry Porsche rejected the scheme on the grounds that it would have made the company too reliant on the Volkswagen/Audi group. Ferry Porsche was understandably proud of the fact that his company had survived as an independent, while others, like Ferrari and Jaguar, had not.

By the mid-1970s Porsche's export markets were well established. Although the USA remained at the top of the export tree, Japan became increasingly important, which was convenient for Porsche as the 911's specification demanded by the USA and Japan were not dissimilar. This 2.7-litre coupe has matt-black trim, colour-coded bumpers and headlamp bezels, and the headlamp lenses are positioned vertically. Under the rear lid there was plenty in the way of exhaust-emissions equipment to sap the power of the flat-six.

With the launch of the 924 and 928 it had become clear to Ferry Porsche that development of the 911 was beginning to lag behind. Senior members of Porsche's management considered that the traditional rear-engined car had had its day, and should be allowed to fade away gracefully. Despite the efforts of a number of people at Zuffenhausen to kick the old girl into touch, the 911 would not quite go away. In 1976 a revised Carrera was launched with a normally aspirated version of the 3-litre turbo unit. Developing 200bhp at 6,000rpm, it was good for 146mph, but not in conditions like this. Snow and ice gave Carrera owners a deep respect for the throttle pedal.

Built in the mid-1970s the Porsche Type 2539 ambulance was the result of a contract from the German Federal Ministry for Research and Technology. Based on Mercedes-Benz and Volkswagen LT Transporters, the brief was basically to create the 'ultimate' ambulance from existing components. Dubbed 'SAVE' (German acronym for Swift ambulance first-aid), the vehicle was fitted with every conceivable piece of equipment a medical team could want, and the chassis, suspension and body unit constructed in such a way that patients were protected from vibrations and road shocks. The engine was a 115bhp Volkswagen/Mercedes diesel unit. An interesting project that demonstrated Porsche's extraordinary talent for providing engineering solutions to everyday problems.

In 1978 Porsche debuted a new version of the 911, the SC, also fitted with the 3-litre engine. Developing 180bhp at 5,500rpm, this version had a top speed of 141mph and 0–60mph acceleration of 6.5 seconds. It was an extremely competent, well-made and fast car but without the dramatic appearance of the 'be-winged' turbo. Conservative Porsche customers considered this to be an advantage; younger folks voiced the opinion that they looked dull.

The Targa version, of course, also soldiered on, but towards the end of the 1970s sales began to tail away. From 1980, the SC had a slight increase in power – to 188bhp – but it appeared that at last the writing was on the wall for the 911. Peter Schutz's appointment to the board, however, halted the 911's decline. Schutz knew little about cars, but a little homework quickly taught him the basic tenets of the company's past success. By the beginning of the 1980s the 911's fortunes would recover – most dramatically.

By the late 1970s Porsche had added the turbocharged version (right) of the 924 to the range. Distinguished externally by the cooling slots in the nosecone, these machines were as fast as the 911SC 3-litre cars, and made for extremely interesting road transport. The factory prepared three 924 turbos for Le Mans in 1980; when Peter Schutz was informed that they stood no chance of outright victory, the American was at a loss to understand what this great company was playing at. The highest-placed 924 on that occasion was sixth overall for Jurgen Barth and Manfred Schurti. A British-entered car, driven by Tony Dron and Andy Rouse, limped home to twelfth place with burnt exhaust valves.

US-spec 911s – a 3-litre SC is seen here – were fitted with fully controlled catalytic converters from 1980, and naturally could only run on unleaded fuels. Several American reporters wrote complimentary road tests about these cars, but their underlying tone was of sentiment and nostalgia for an old friend, rather than prosaic and wild excitement for the 'latest Porsche'. With a welcome return to the Fuchs alloy wheels – ('cookie-cutters' were also available), matt-black trim and a 'whale-tale', these cars are now correctly considered as classics among Porsches.

In 1981 the 'basic' 3-litre 911SC had yet another increase in engine output – to 204bhp – and top speed rose to a perfectly respectable 146mph. Acceleration to 60mph from rest took a minimum of 5.7 seconds, but good as these figures undoubtedly were, the most remarkable facet of the 911 at this time was the timeless shape of the body which, in essence, had not changed since the debut of the 901 in 1963.

After a degree of success with the 924s at Le Mans in 1980 Porsche launched the Carrera GT version, a purposeful machine with wide wheel arches and 911-style Fuchs five-spoke alloy wheels. For sports-car traditionalists it was a most desirable, if expensive, projectile with 150mph performance potential, and to the classic front-engined, rear-wheel drive layout. Many Porsche enthusiasts warmed to these cars – 911 owners found them 'interesting' – but they just lacked the 911's innate character.

Works Porsche driver and five times Le Mans winner Derek Bell, seen here with organiser of the now defunct Birmingham Superprix, Dave Lucas, had a special road version of the Carrera GT for personal use. With its appropriate registration plate the car was much modified – engine power was not publicly disclosed – and had Perspex headlamp lenses in place of the regular, concealed, 'pop-up' units. The bonnet was also attached with Dzeus fasteners. The mighty 'Dinger' once told this author that the car was 'great fun', which roughly translated from 'Dinger-speak' means that it was 'hellish quick'.

Peter Schutz's response to Porsche's plans to close 911 production down by the beginning of the 1980s resulted in this special design study. The first true Porsche cabriolet since the days of the 356, the car was exhibited at the 1981 Frankfurt Auto Show to test public reaction. It was, as Schutz and Ferry Porsche expected, rather favourable, and plans for a production version were put into immediate effect.

The first production cabriolet versions of the 911 were available in 3-litre form from 1983. In one sense it set the Porsche scene for many years ahead because it was not only seen as a hugely exciting sports car, with performance aplenty, but as a symbol of a quietly confident lifestyle. It was an understatement of good taste and discerning choice that appealed to the kind of people who considered Lamborghinis and, to a lesser extent, Ferraris, as the personification of automotive vulgarity.

By contrast with the utterly gorgeous 911 cabriolet, there was nothing particularly subtle or understated about special versions of the 924 turbo supplied to the German police force. Kitted with flashing lights, sirens, horns and loud-hailers, these cars, like all previous Porsche police cars, served a useful purpose on the country's extensive autobahn network. With a top speed in the region of 150mph, there was not much to defeat a 924 turbo on public roads, although a few 911 turbo owners regularly proved otherwise.

Along with the 911 cabrio, Porsche developed the 956 Group C racing car during the early 1980s. Success at Le Mans in 1982, where the Rothmans-sponsored cars placed first, second and third, first time out of the box, marked the beginning of a new era for the company. The 956, and long-wheelbase 962 development car, would become the most successful sports racer in the history of motor racing. Victories and other high placings were monotonous throughout the 1980s, the ensuing publicity being largely responsible for reviving the fortunes of the company's road cars. Driven by Belgian Jacky Ickx, the 956 seen here is at the Esses, Le Mans, 1985, an event won by the similar Joest-entered car of Klaus Ludwig and Paola Barilla. Jochen Dauer and Vern Schuppan both made a small number of road versions of these cars.

In addition to Porsche's track activities, the company prepared for an assault on the 1984 Paris–Dakar Raid. For this unusual event Porsche used 3.2-litre versions of the Carrera, with raised and reinforced suspension and four-wheel drive. On the face of it the 911 was not a particularly suitable mount to cope with the rough and tumble of the Sahara Desert, notwithstanding a close shave with victory in past East African Safaris, but René Metge came up trumps to score a well-deserved win.

In 1984 Porsche also introduced the new 3.2-litre engine into the road-going 911 Carrera. With a maximum of 231bhp at 5,900rpm, it was an eminently usable and exciting piece of equipment, with a top speed in the region of 155mph and utterly 'wild' mid-range acceleration. With a reputation for being almost unbreakable, many examples of these cars, despite high mileages, are still in regular use and continue to give reliable service.

From 1981 Porsche built several different versions of the 'Flachbau' (flat-nose) 911 turbo. Inspired by the 935 sports racing cars of the late 1970s, the 911's normal headlamps were dispensed with and 'pop-up' units were sunk into the modified wings in their place. While the front wings were in zinc-coated steel, much of the front end was made of lightweight glassfibre and the aesthetic effect was nothing less than dramatic.

Mansour Ojjeh, head of the Paris-based company TAG, which sponsored the Porsche-built McLaren Formula 1 turbo engine, commissioned this 3.3-litre Flachbau turbo in 1983. Painted in a deep shade of red, its resemblance to the 935 racing car is apparent; there is a deep chin spoiler at the front, huge 'bi-plane' rear wing and vents in the tops of the front wings to allow air from under the wheel arches to escape.

A car fit for a king, literally, this Flachbau was built specially for the late King Hussein of Jordan. Hussein of Jordan was a great car and motorcycle fanatic, who kept a large collection of Porsches, Mercedes and Italian exotica, mostly at his English residence. One of the King's great pleasures was to don leathers and a full-face helmet and blast, unrecognised, down the M4 motorway during his visits to Britain.

A development of the Audi-built 924, the 944 was added to the Porsche range in 1981 – at first as a 'tin-top' coupe. A car of which Ferry Porsche approved, this was an all-Porsche effort, and fitted with a 2.5-litre, four-cylinder engine. To overcome the inherent vibration and lack of balance in a large-capacity four-cylinder, Porsche balanced the crankshaft with two contra-rotating shafts. This system was first devised by Lanchester; as applied to the Porsche, the big 'four' was as smooth as a conventional six-cylinder power unit.

Homage to the 1960 RS60 Porsche, and predating the advent of the Boxster in the mid-1990s, this wonderful creation, from the 1980s, was the work of Herr Hagemann, the well-known 'Porschephile'. A unique car, with alloy bodywork faithfully copied from the original, it was based on 911 components and sports a flat-six in the rear. The modern, wide-rimmed 911 wheels give the game away that this is not a genuine RS60. Performance is said to be of a 'shattering' nature . . . which is hardly surprising.

One of many experimental vehicles built at Zuffenhausen down the years, this prototype was constructed in 1987. Primarily intended for testing aerodynamics, it bears an uncanny resemblance to Derek Bell's 924 Carrera on p. 114. The rear wing is interesting, because one of similar style and function was fitted to the contemporary Group B Porsche 959, the most sophisticated of the 1980s supercars.

After Porsche's success with the 959 on the Paris–Dakar Raid, and a foray to Le Mans with the 961 racing version, the company launched the 959 as a pure road car. With permanent four-wheel drive, twin turbochargers and 450bhp from the 2,847cc flat-six the car's road ability was never in question. Its complexities, price tag and top speed of close to 200mph took the concept of a sports car beyond the imaginations of even seasoned motoring folk (as did the bills for maintenance), and just 283 found lucky owners before production was halted in 1988.

Porsche followed the 959 in 1988 with the Speedster, a model that revived the name and memories of the original 356 Speedster of the mid-1950s. Fitted with the 3.2-litre flat-six the 911 Speedster closely aped the minimalist theme of the 356 version. The car's most distinctive feature was its short, but immensely strong, steeply raked windscreen and rear tonneau cover. Particularly popular in the USA, the car was an extremely powerful styling statement that harked back to Porsche's past and paved the way for other manufacturers to capitalise on the 'retro-look'.

This version of the Speedster, with an all-enveloping, wind-cheating cockpit tonneau, was shown at the 1987 Frankfurt Auto Show as a design study, but, regrettably, did not go into production. Such devices are reminiscent of so many sports cars of the 1950s, fitted with cockpit tonneaus, in many cases for the purpose of achieving higher speeds down Mulsanne at Le Mans. In recent times this glorious stretch of public road, where the Porsche 917s once attained speeds in excess of 240mph, has been completely altered by the introduction of two artificial chicanes. These are considered by some to be a safety measure, aimed at slowing cars down, whereas many drivers – the people who actually know about safety at Le Mans – curse these new additions. Previously, Mulsanne gave drivers the only chance of a rest from the constant strain of braking and accelerating around the rest of the course; the chicanes merely add to the strain.

To mark the eightieth birthday of the company's helmsman, Ferry Porsche, who remained as active and interested in cars as ever, Porsche built this most interesting 911 in 1989 as a design study. Dubbed the 'Panamericana', after Porsche's success in the great Mexican road races of the 1950s, the car was unique, had a streamlined, tapering glass area and flanks shaped to direct the airflow from behind the front wheels to the tops of the rear wings. A birthday present that anyone would be glad to receive!

Unlike so many design studies exhibited on the annual motor show circus, the Panamericana was not a mock-up built for the purpose of encouraging journalists to write headlines about 'cars of the future', but a real machine that could be, and frequently was, driven. The shape of the rear end and taillamps are both similar to the fifth generation 911 (codenamed 996), launched in 1997. Note the unique six-spoke, alloy wheels.

By the end of the 1980s the 911's fortunes had been well and truly revived and were riding high. Attempts to kill the car off were wholly thwarted, principally thanks to Peter Schutz and Ferry Porsche, neither of whom really believed that the front-engined Porsches were worthy replacements. The classic 'be-winged' cars that had served the company so well from the mid-1970s, however, had, to all intents and purposes, outlived their usefulness after so many years of development and production.

The increasing popularity of the 911 Cabriolet would eventually see the end of the classic Targa; the styling of the former gave the car a much more integrated and harmonious shape, while to some, the Targa's roll-hoop had always looked 'fussy' and incongruous. Along with its coupe sister, this particular model, however, had also outlived its useful life, both cars bowing out in 1989 to make way for a new generation 911.

Launched in 1989, the new, third-generation 911, although ostensibly the same as ever, was a wholly new car having been designed on a fresh piece of paper, or more accurately a computer screen. Codenamed 964, the new car had ABS braking, came with a choice of traditional rear- or permanent four-wheel drive (Carrera 4) and seven-spoke, 'star-shaped', alloy wheels. Slung out in the tail was a revised version of the air-cooled flat-six – pushed out to 3.6 litres – and no less than 250bhp developed at a maximum of 6,100rpm.

Open-top models in the Porsche line-up included the 911 cabriolet and Targa, and the 944 Cabriolet. This official 1990 publicity shot portrays the mood of the 1980s in colour. Porsche, like so many other manufacturers, used sombre, conservative shades throughout much of this economically troubled decade. It was a period in which the well heeled became mindful of the need to play their cards close to their chest. Owning expensive cars, painted in dull colours, was but one way that many attempted to blend into the scenery without raising the ire of the 'have-nots'.

One particularly interesting innovation, first seen on the Volkswagen Corrado in 1989, was the rear spoiler, which was automatically deployed at about 120km/h – when it is actually needed – and retracted at 60km/h. By comparison with the 'whale-tails' of the past the new device was small, but worked well enough and was less susceptible to the activities of vandals when the car was parked.

As the 1990s unfolded bright bold colours returned to the automotive world, a proven sign of economic prosperity and growth. This American-spec RS, photographed at speed, retained a revised version of the 'whale-tail' rear spoiler, complete with the traditional chunky rubber piece around the sides and back.

Between 1993 and 1994 Porsche produced just 1,875 examples of the 3.6-litre turbo, which, apart from looking rather purposeful, had performance potential that ordinary mortals had not a hope in hell of exploring to the full. Developing 360bhp at 5,500rpm, the powerful engine was capable of propelling the car to 175mph, and to 60mph from a standing start in 4.7 seconds. These figures are, of course, utterly meaningless; Porsche would go on to make even faster cars but, by the time most folks can afford to buy such hell-raising machines, the passage of a week seems to be too fast – never mind travelling at 175mph!

The 3.6-litre turbo was also available in Flachbau format, but this version made less of a styling statement than the original 935-inspired Flachbaus of the past. The 964's large front and rear bumpers gave the entire range something of a 'flabby' appearance, and the angled headlamps hinted at an affinity with the front-engined 928. Controversial styling or not this was one hellishly quick Porsche . . .

. . . as was the 'ordinary' European-spec Carrera RS which, with 260bhp from the 3.6-litre engine, was 10bhp more than the regular Carrera 2/4s. Performance was not quite in the turbo's league, but sufficient to frighten stupid anyone who had previously driven nothing more powerful than a Vauxhall Astra! This fine study, from Porsche's official archive, shows an RS under hard cornering, its stiff suspension giving just a hint of body lean and supple, confident ride.

A bright-red Speedster, 1993. Fitted with the regular 3.6-litre, 250bhp engine, this rudimentary ragtop was a genuine 160mph flier built to Carrera 2 specification, but with all the usual Speedster hallmarks. Note the twin headrest fairings, and those ghastly colour-keyed alloy wheels.

Two delectable cars from Porsche in 1993, the 968 Turbo S (the 944's replacement) and 911 Carrera RS. The former was an extremely well-engineered, beautifully balanced sports car with 160mph performance potential but, despite healthy sales, never captured public imagination like the 'hot' Carreras. This particular example was 1 of just 129 produced in 1993, and was fitted with a special 3.8-litre, atmospherically aspirated version of the flat-six. Developing 300bhp at 6,500rpm, it boasted a top speed of 168mph, and 0–60mph acceleration of 4.9 seconds – without the drawback of the small amount of throttle 'lag' characteristic of the turbo model. Note the revisions to the 911's rear wing.

As with so many past Carreras, Porsche intended the 3.8-litre car as a road-legal machine that could be taken to a circuit and raced competitively in GT competition. To this end the company also produced this special RSR ('R' for racing) lightweight version, stripped of superfluous equipment. From a legal point of view there was nothing to prevent these cars being driven on public roads but, in the manner of so many competition machines nowadays, the majority were dragged to race meetings in the hold of a transporter.

One of the most astounding cars of the 1990s, the Audi Avant RS 2 was launched in 1993/1994 to the astonishment of the entire motoring world. Built by Audi these special machines were sent, unfinished, to the Porsche factory for tuning purposes. The result of Porsche's labour was a five-cylinder, twenty-valve, turbocharged estate car, with seating for five, capable of 163mph and 0–60mph in 5.4 seconds. The 2,226cc engine developed a remarkable 315bhp, with 911 brakes and 'Cup' alloy wheels to prevent the beast from getting into spots of unwelcome bother. Included in the specification was a six-speed gearbox, from the Audi S2, permanent four-wheel drive and truly astounding fuel consumption – 36.7mpg was attainable at a constant 56mph. Note the purposeful air intakes in the front bumper.

In 1994 Porsche launched the fourth-generation 911 – the 993 in Porsche's numbering hierarchy – and in doing so created what many continue to regard as the finest of all 911s. The restyling exercise was nothing less than dramatic, but combined the simple beauty of Butzi Porsche's original 1963 penmanship with 'cutey' chic and the demands made by modern aerodynamic thinking.

By 1993 it was all over for the third generation of 911s as production of the 964 was halted to make way for a revised breed. For devotees of atmospherically-aspirated engines this 3.8-litre Carrera RS was, arguably, the best of the third-generation roadgoing 964s. With its 17 in wheels and 'bi-plane' rear wing, the Carrera's appearance was every bit as dramatic as its shattering performance. It is also interesting that the use of yellow paint had become more widespread in the 1990s than

previously; yellow cars had all but died out in the 1980s for the simple reason that this colour was heavily dependent on the use of lead in its chemical make-up. Volkswagen, however, discovered a satisfactory method of mixing yellow without lead, and were quick to point out that yellow versions of the Corrado (launched in 1989) were the world's first yellow cars without lead in their paintwork.

This rear 'three-quarter' view of the 993 admirably illustrates complete styling synthesis; there is not one part of the car that has an incorrect angle, or awkward shape or line anywhere. Apart from acutely brilliant styling, though, there were sub-cutaneous improvements, including revised rear suspension that genuinely improved the car's handling. Carrera 2 and 4 models were powered by a revised 3.6-litre flat-six developing 272bhp at 6,100rpm, sufficient to propel both versions to an almost completely academic top speed of 168mph.

Some 170kg lighter than the standard 911s, the Carrera 'Cup' cars brought the racing series well and truly alive with the advent of the 993. Despite the standard fitment of the road version's three-way catalytic converter, these cars developed no less than 310bhp to 315bhp from 1997 – and were responsible for some of Europe's closest and most exciting track battles since the days of the BMW 'Batmobiles' and Cologne-built Ford Capris of the 1970s.

It could be argued that a racing car has no place whatever in a book about Porsche road cars, but there is a perfectly valid case for the defence. From the earliest days of the 356 – indeed from the very first Porsche prototype of the late 1940s – Porsche's road cars were intended as dual-purpose, race-cum-shopping machines. It would be a fairly noisy experience, but the 'Cup' Carreras were so tractable that they could, in theory, be used for journeys to the shops. This is also a totally unashamed example of non-objective, self-indulgent bias on the part of the author – a real sucker for black racing Porsches! Note that Supercup cars sported large rear wings from 1995.

The squat lines of the 993 cabriolet's profile are shown to good effect in this perfectly lit publicity shot. People are conspicuously

absent, but the deep blue Mediterranean sky and cypress trees tell a story of a 'dream' lifestyle – a reality for the lucky few.

Launched in 1996, the mid-engine Boxster harks back to the RSK 718 of the late 1950s, and is one of Porsche's most successful cars. With 204bhp from the 2.5-litre engine, the car has a top speed of 149mph, business-like acceleration – 0–60mph in 6.7 seconds – and an exhaust note above 4,000rpm that sounds like something akin to a set of bagpipes being ventilated by a particularly nasty hurricane. In every respect it is a stunning car, and every inch a Porsche, but the production model caused Porsche's press department in Stuttgart something of a headache. The prototype Boxster, pictures of which appeared widely in the international press, was an extremely pretty car. By comparison, the production version was bland, and Porsche are understandably fed up with critics pointing this out to them.

Painted in the classic German colour combination of silver highlighted with touches of red, this Carrera 4S debuted in 1996. Bristling with luxury equipment, it was, at 1,450kg, a full 30kg heavier than the 'standard' Carrera 4. Fitted with the 285bhp version of the 3.6-litre engine, introduced in 1996, its top speed of 168mph did not compare favourably with the Carrera 4's 172mph, but at this velocity the difference does not matter, except to car-mad schoolboys who continue to argue among themselves about 'the best car in the world, mate'.

Regrettably, the pretty 993 remained in production for all too short a time, and was replaced in 1997 by the fifth-generation 996. Arguably the world's safest and most technically advanced sports cars, the 911's parentage is self-evident, but although the flat-six is still in the right place, it is water-cooled for the first time. A 3.4-litre unit, which in Carrera guise develops 300bhp at 6,600rpm, it is considerably quieter than the classic air-cooled 'six'. In principle, 911 fans begrudingly approve of the latest incarnation, but usually get completely hooked after a blast to 180mph and back.

The GT1 must surely rank as one of the most beautifully proportioned and stylish sports cars ever made. It is for no other purpose than driving at high speed in complete safety. Luggage space is minimal, sound insulation from engine noise in the cabin is virtually non-existent and the seats are not conducive to use as a 'passion-wagon'. By the time the world's other

sports-car manufacturers have caught up with this kind of motoring technology, Porsche will have advanced even further – an intriguing thought that beggars belief.

In 1996 Porsches filled the top three places at Le Mans, winning both the GT1 and GT2 classes into the bargain. There was another outright victory at the Sarthe in 1997. In celebration the company made this totally intoxicating road version of the 911 GT1 for a small number of people, of a kind that do not need to be concerned with the financial tribulations of normal folk. A 1990s state-of-the-art road sports car, it goes without saying that the GT1 is Porsche's idea of the ultimate driving machine. Its top speed? Roughly 20–30mph above that at which a Boeing 747 becomes airborne.

The 1998 street version of the GT1 Le Mans car utilises headlamps from the 996 road car, a narrower cockpit and broader sidepods. With more than 600bhp, braking power that cannot be imagined, roadholding that is idiot-proof at virtually any speed and running costs that are capable of making grand Lottery winners grind their teeth and regret the day that they sold their 1.3-litre Ford Escorts, this formidable machine is a representation of fifty years of Porsche know-how. As such it is just about perfect.

A 2-litre 'screamer' – the original 911 – in its natural setting. Dawn is breaking, a long straight road lies ahead for many miles and there is nothing to do except kick seven bells out of the throttle pedal. Life could sometimes be this tough in the good ol' days . . .

PORSCHE 911 PRODUCTION RECORD

Year	Model	Numbers
1963	901	13
1964–7	911 (2.0)	10,723
1965–9	912	30,300
1967–9	911S (2.0)	5,056
1968–9	911T (2.0)	6,318
1968	911L (2.0)	11,610
1969	911E (2.0)	2,826
1970–1	911T (2.2)	15,082
1970–1	911E (2.2)	4,927
1970–1	911S (2.2)	4,691
1972–3	911T (2.4)	16,933
1972–3	911E (2.4)	4,406
1972–3	911S (2.4)	5,094
1973	Carrera RS	1,590
1974	Carrera RS (3.0)	109
1974–5	911(2.7)	9,360
1976–7	911 (2.7)	7,900
1974–7	911S (2.7)	17,124
1974–5	Carrera (2.7)	3,353
1974–7	Turbo (3.0)	3,227
1975	912E	2,099
1978–9	Turbo (3.3)	17,425
1978–83	911SC (3.0)	57,972
1984–9	Carrera (3.2)	49,289
1984	911SC-RS	20
1987	959	283
1987–9	911 Club Sport	340
1989–93	Carrera 2/4	56,363
1991	Carrera 2 RS	2,364
1991–2	Turbo (3.6)	4,107
1992	Turbo S (3.6)	80
1993	Carrera RS (3.8)	129

Year	Model	Numbers
1993–4	Turbo (3.6)	1,875
1994–8	Carrera/4 (3.6)	34,396
1994–6	993 Cup (3.7)	327
1995–6	Carrera RS(3.7)	1,123
1995–7	Turbo (3.6)	8,919
1996–7	Carrera (3.6)	34,846

Appendix II

PORSCHE MOTORSPORT ACHIEVEMENTS

Two outright victories in the Paris–Dakar Raid

Three IMSA Supercar Championships

Three Formula 1 World Championship victories in partnership with McLaren

Four outright victories in the Monte-Carlo Rally

Six German National Championships

Eleven outright victories in the Targa Florio

Fourteen World Championship of Makes/World Team Championships

Sixteen outright victories at Le Mans

Seventeen outright victories in the Sebring 12 Hours

Eighteen outright victories in the Daytona 24 Hours

Twenty European Hillclimb Championships

More than 23,000 victories in total

Appendix III

PORSCHE SAFETY DEVELOPMENTS

1955	First German car with a laminated windscreen
1956	Lap belt
1962	Three-point seat belts
1964	Safety steering system
1969	Integrated head restraints. Experiments with ABS and use of drilled brake discs in racing applications

1970	Four-piston brake calipers used in racing
1971	Galvanised floor panels
1972	Automatic three-point belts
1973	First plastic fuel tank in a German production car, flame-resistant interior trim and side-impact reinforcement in US-spec cars
1975	First vehicle worldwide with fully galvanised body. Drilled brake discs and four-piston brake callipers fitted to production Porsches
1982	Underbody design with ground-effect and tyre-pressure monitoring in racing cars
1983	ABS fitted to production cars
1984	Four-wheel drive in racing cars
1985	Door reinforcement fitted to production models worldwide
1986	Four-wheel drive, ground-effect underbody and tyre-pressure monitoring on production models
1987	First European manufacturer to fit twin airbags in USA
1991	First manufacturer to fit twin airbags as standard on home market
1993	Multi-link lightweight axle with sub-frame fitted to production models
1995	On-board diagnosis and 18-in hollow-spoke wheels fitted to production cars
1996	Monobloc brakes fitted to production cars
1997	Porsche Side Impact System (**POSIP**) fitted to production cars

Appendix IV

PORSCHE 911 PERFORMANCE

Year	Model	Max Power	Top Speed	0–62mph (seconds)
1963	901	130bhp	131mph	8.5
1964–7	911 (2.0)	130bhp	130mph	8.3
1965–9	912	90bhp	119mph	11.1
1967–9	911S (2.0)	160bhp	137mph	8.0
1968–9	911T (2.0)	110bhp	124mph	8.3
1968	911L (2.0)	130bhp	131mph	10.6
1969	911E (2.0)	140bhp	134mph	8.4
1970–1	911T (2.2)	125bhp	127mph	9.5
1970–1	911E (2.2)	155bhp	137mph	7.6
1970–1	911S (2.2)	180bhp	138mph	7.0
1972–3	911T (2.4)	130bhp	127mph	8.1
1972–3	911E (2.4)	165bhp	138mph	7.9
1972–3	911S (2.4)	190bhp	144mph	6.6
1973	Carrera	210bhp	152mph	5.8
1974	Carrera (3.0)	230bhp	148mph	4.9

Year	Model	Max Power	Top Speed	0–62mph (seconds)
1974–5	911 (2.7)	150bhp	131mph	7.9
1976–7	911 (2.7)	165bhp	135mph	7.8
1974–7	911S (2.7)	175bhp	142mph	6.1
1974–5	Carrera (2.7)	210bhp	150mph	6.3
1974–7	Turbo (3.0)	260bhp	155mph	6.0
1976–7	Carrera (3.0)	200bhp	146mph	6.1
1975	912E (2.0)	90bhp	115mph	11.3
1978–89	Turbo (3.3)	300bhp	162mph	5.1
1978–9	911SC(3.0)	180bhp	141mph	6.5
1980	911SC (3.0)	188bhp	141mph	7.0
1981–3	911SC (3.0)	204bhp	146mph	5.7
1984–9	Carrera (3.2)	231bhp	152mph	5.6
1984	911 SC-RS (3.0)	255bhp	159mph	5.0
1987	959 (2.8)	450bhp	199mph	3.7
1987–9	911 Club Sport	231bhp	156mph	5.6
1989–93	Carrera 2/4	250bhp	162mph	5.7
1991	Carrera 2 RS	260bhp	162mph	5.3
1991–2	Turbo (3.6)	320bhp	168mph	5.0
1992	Turbo S (3.6)	381bhp	180mph	4.6
1993	Carrera RS (3.8)	300bhp	168mph	4.9
1993–4	Turbo (3.6)	360bhp	175mph	4.8
1994–5	Carrera (3.6)	272bhp	168mph	5.6
1995	Carrera 4 (3.6)	272bhp	168mph	5.3
1994–6	993 Cup (3.7)	315bhp	175mph	4.7
1995–6	Carrera RS (3.7)	300bhp	172mph	5.0
1995–7	Turbo (3.6)	408bhp	180mph	4.5
1996–7	Carrera (3.6)	285bhp	171mph	5.4
1996–7	Carrera Tip (3.6)	285bhp	168mph	6.4
1996–7	Carrera 4 (3.6)	285bhp	171mph	5.3
1996–7	Carrera 4S (3.6)	285bhp	168mph	5.3
1997	Carrera S (3.6)	285bhp	168mph	5.4
1998	Carrera (3.4)	300bhp	174mph	5.2

Appendix V

PORSCHE UNIT FIGURES

Porsche production models: 71

Porsche model variants: 135

Porsche racing cars: 102

Porsche production sports cars: 46

Third-party development projects: in excess of 2,000

Patents: in excess of 11,500 since 1931

Appendix VI

PORSCHE COMPETITION SUCCESS

1951 Porsche debuts at Le Mans. The 356 driven by Auguste Veuillet and Edmond Mouche is victorious in the 1100cc class and romps home in twentieth position. Paul von Guilleaume places third and wins the 1500cc class on the Liège–Rome–Liège Rally, with Huschke von Hantsein second in the 1100cc class. An 1100cc 356 sets new speed records at 100mph at Montlhéry over 500 miles, 1,000km and 6 hours

1952 Count Johnny Lurani wins 1500cc class in a 356 in the Mille Miglia. Polensky and Schluter take outright victory in a 1500cc 356 on the Liège–Rome–Liège. Veuillet and Mouche repeat their victory in the 1100cc class at Le Mans in a 356

1953 The von Frankenburg/Frere 356 win the 1500cc class at Le Mans, beating the similar car of Herrmann/Glöckler by 900m

1954 Porsche win both the 1100cc and 1500cc classes at Le Mans. Maleric and Cerne take a 356 to outright victory on the Acropolis Rally in Greece. The 550 Spyder claims the top four places in the Grand Prix of Europe at the Nürburgring

1955 Porsche 550 Spyders place fourth, fifth and sixth overall at Le Mans

1956 In a single-handed drive Umberto Maglioli scores a convincing victory on the Targa Florio in a 550 Spyder. A similar 550 wins the 1500cc class at Le Mans and places fifth overall

1957 Edgar Barth is victorious in an RS Spyder in the Nürburgring F2 race

1958 Jean Behra wins the Mont Ventoux Hillclimb and F2 race at Rheims in a Spyder. Porsche RSKs place third, fourth and fifth overall at Le Mans

1959 Porsche win the Targa Florio outright for the second time, but all six Porsches entered for Le Mans fail to finish

1960 Bonnier and Herrmann score Porsche's third outright victory in the Targa Florio. Stirling Moss wins the South African Grand Prix in Rob Walker's privately entered F2 Porsche

1961 Giancarlo Baghetti wins the F2 Rome Grand Prix in a Porsche

1962 Dan Gurney wins the French Grand Prix at Rouen in the 804 Porsche F1 car, and again a fortnight later in the non-championship round at Solitude. Porsche retire from Grand Prix racing at the end of the season

1963 Bonnier and Abate score Porsche's fourth outright victory on the Targa Florio in an eight-cylinder 718/8 sports car

1964 Baron Pucci and Colin Davis take the new fibreglass-bodied 904 GT car to victory in the Targa Florio. A 904 wins the 2-litre class at Le Mans

1965 Herbert Linge and Peter Falk take the 2-litre class and fifth place overall in the Monte-Carlo Rally in a 911. Linge and Peter Nocker score fourth at Le Mans in a 904/6

1966 Willy Mairesse and Herbert Müller in a 906 score Porsche's sixth outright victory in the Targa Florio. 906s take fourth to seventh places at Le Mans

1967 Vic Elford and David Stone win the GT class in the Monte-Carlo Rally

1968   Elford/Stone take a 911 to outright victory in the Monte-Carlo Rally. Porsche 907s take first and second places at Daytona, first at Sebring and Elford scores victory in the Targa Florio in a 907.

1969   The formidable 917 debuts but proves unreliable at first. Jo Siffert and Brian Redman win five rounds of the World Sports Car Championship in a 908, but are narrowly beaten to the title by Ford. Bjorn Waldegaard and Lars Helmer win the Monte-Carlo and Swedish Rallies in a 911

1970   A 917 is taken to victory at Le Mans, Porsche's first outright win at the Sarthe. Waldegaard and Helmer take a 911 to victory in the Monte-Carlo and Swedish Rallies, again in a 911. Works-backed JW 917s win the World Endurance Championship, and Siffert and Redman score another Porsche victory in the Targa Florio in a 908

1971   Outright victory for Porsche at Le Mans again with a 917. The JW Automotive Porsche team take the Endurance Championship for the second time

1972   A turbocharged 917 Spyder wins Can-Am Championship

1973   A revised 917 Spyder develops 1,100bhp and, in Mark Donohue's hands, completely dominates the Can-Am Championship. Peter Gregg and Hurley Haywood win the Daytona 24 Hours in a 911 RSR. Müller and Van Lennep score Porsche's eleventh outright victory in the Targa Florio

1974–5   Porsche build the 911 Turbo for the forthcoming World Championship for Manufacturers

1976   Porsche take the Championship for Manufacturers with a 935, the World Sports Car Championship with a 936 and the European GT Championship with a 934. Ickx and Van Lennep win Le Mans in a 936

1977   Porsche take the World Championship for Manufacturers with a 935. Ickx, Haywood and Barth win Le Mans in a 936, Porsche's fourth outright victory in the French classic

1978   Jean-Pierre Nicholas wins the Monte-Carlo Rally in a 911. Peter Gregg takes the IMSA Camel GT category in a 935 and Porsche win the World Championship for Manufacturers for the third time

1979   A 935 entered by Erwin and Manfred Kremer, and driven by Klaus Ludwig and the Whittington brothers, wins Le Mans

1980   USAC changes indycar rules and renders Porsche's new single-seater contender useless over night. Reinhold Joest, Rolf Stommelen and Volkert Merl take a 935 to victory in the Daytona 24 Hours

1981   Jacky Ickx and Derek Bell take a 936 to victory at Le Mans

1982   Porsche 956 ground-effect cars score first, second and third at Le Mans, and win the World Endurance Championship

1983   Porsches fill nine of the top ten places at Le Mans; a BMW is placed ninth. Porsche take the World Endurance Championship – again

1984   Porsche win all rounds of the WEC including Le Mans. Rene Metge wins the Paris–Dakar Raid in a four-wheel-drive 911

1985   Reinhold Joest's privately entered 956 wins Le Mans driven by Klaus Ludwig, Paolo Barilla and 'Jon Winter'. Hans-Joachim Stuck and Derek Bell win the Group C Championship in a 956, but Porsche drivers Manfred Winkelhock and Stefan Bellof are involved in fatal crashes

1986   Derek Bell, Al Holbert and Al Unser jnr win Daytona in a Porsche. Bell, Holbert and Stuck go on to win Le Mans. Rene Metge wins the Paris–Dakar Raid in a Porsche 959

1987   Bell, Holbert and Robinson win at Daytona, with Bell, Holbert and Stuck taking outright victory at Le Mans again in a 962. This is Porsche's twelfth outright win at Le Mans, and the fourth successive win in a 24-hour race for Derek Bell and Al Holbert

1988   A disastrous year for Porsche as a Jaguar takes victory at Le Mans. The German company prepares a new single-seater for Indycar racing, but team director Al Holbert dies in an aeroplane crash in September

1989   Bob Wollek and Frank Jelinski score a shock victory in Reinhold Joest's 962 at Dijon, beating the Sauber-Mercedes and Jaguars. Derek Bell, Bob Wollek and John Andretti take a 962 to victory in the Daytona 24 Hours

1990   Porsches finish third and fourth at Le Mans to a pair of winning Jaguars, a bleak day indeed for Porsche fans

1991   Bob Wollek, Hurley Haywood, Frank Jelinski, Henri Pescarolo and 'Jon Winter' take a Joest 962 to outright victory in the Daytona 24 Hours

1992/3   Porsche lie dormant and wait for the return of GT racing

1994   Based on the 962, special Jochen Dauer Porsches are prepared for Le Mans, and finish first and third

1995   BMW-powered McLaren F1s dominate the World Sports Championship and outclass the Porsches to win Le Mans

1996   The 911 GT1 debuts at Le Mans, but is beaten by a Joest prototype Porsche. Porsche GT1s win at Brands Hatch, Spa and Zhuhai

1997   McLaren and Mercedes-Benz share victories in all rounds of the endurance championship, except Le Mans, where a Joest prototype is all-conquering. This is the fifteenth victory by a Porsche at the French circuit

1998   Porsche produces a new GT1, and wins Le Mans yet again

1999   Porsches are ever present but a BMW (built by Williams Engineering in Britain) wins Le Mans.

INDEX